The Faces of God

The Faces of God

Canaanite Mythology as Hebrew Theology

Jacob Rabinowitz

Dedicated

to

Aharon Amir

Poet, Patriot, Canaanite

Copyright 1998 by Spring Publications. All rights reserved. First Printing 1991.
Published by Spring Publications, Woodstock CT.

The cover image is "Constellation Draco" from *Theatrum Mundi* by Giovanni Paolo Gallucci (Venice, 1588).

Cover designed and produced by the Tanuki Arts Group.

Printed in Canada

Rabinowitz, Jacob
    The Faces of God, Canaanite mythology as Hebrew Theology / Jacob Rabinowitz
      p.   cm
      Includes bibliographical references
      ISBN 0-88214 117-1 (paperback)
      1. Bible. O.T. -- Criticism, interpretation, &c. 2. Gods, Canaanite. 3. God -- Biblical teaching. 4. Mythology, Canaanite -- Influence. 5. Middle Eastern literature -- Relation to the Old Testament. I. Title.
    BS 1192.6.R33   1998
    221.6'6--dc21   98-22427
                                                              CIP

Table of Contents:

Introduction 11

Historical Overview 17

Chapter One: El 27

Chapter Two: Baal 37

Chapter Three: The Center 63

Chapter Four: Asherah and Anat 83

Conclusion 97

Appendix: Literary Renderings 99

Bibliography 115

Introduction

Scientific Bible Criticism

The *Anchor Bible Dictionary* (1992), which is something of a summation of biblical research at the end of the 20th century, doesn't *have* an article on Israelite religion. It begins the topic with a treatment of Rabbinic Judaism. Even the article on Israel's early history is essentially a survey of the problems the subject presents. The entire topic of the faith from Abraham on is so hotly disputed that no single book can be pointed to as expressing the concensus of serious scholarship. And with good reason.

Israel's archaeology is, in comparison with that of Greece or Egypt, very poor. Adequate corroborating evidence for the textual accounts is simply not there. Nor did Israel's neighbors take much note of her in their historical record. In addition, the Hebrew Bible itself is like a patchwork quilt: almost all its component books are made up of fragments. Indeed, it is a patchwork quilt made from other patchwork quilts: there are layers, not only of source material, but of editing. A final problem is the size of the Bible: for a thousand year period (1200 to 200 BC, a stretch as long as all of Classical antiquity) we have only this collection of texts, which is roughly as long as the works of Plato.[1]

In this century two major approaches to the texts have predominated. One the one hand, the archaeological (e.g., Albright, de Vaux), which has confirmed the historicity of various details (e.g., place names, details of material culture) in a way that encourages belief in the Bible's documentary verity, though the support is too diffuse to settle many of the most pressing questions.

On the other hand, we have the "text analysis" (*traditionsgeschichtliche*) school, exemplified by Alt, Noth, &c., which attempts to account for every discrepancy in the text by a divergent historical fact (e.g., the name change

---

1. There are of course the ancient Near Eastern parallels which Pritchard has presented in his famous anthology, but none of these were drawn on in the same participatory way that the Romans borrowed from Greek literature.

from Abram to Abraham could indicate a reconciliation of geographically and thus linguistically differing traditions about one patriarch, or even the conflation of stories about two patriarchs). This approach, which presently holds the field, has a tendency to make the personalities of even such major figures as Moses seemingly fragment — if not evaporate.

Since the 70's, Old Testament studies have, despite factual gains from archaeology, Semitic philology, &c., and an increasing agreement as to where the difficulties lie, reached a sort of *aporia* as a final result of the super-sceptical tendencies of text-criticism, which were in turn exacerbated by difficulties raised by the Ugaritic material. Hence the terrible reticence of the *Anchor Bible Dictionary,* and every other survey that seeks to be authoritative. Even for the Kingdom period and on up to the beginnings of Rabbinic Judaism, where the sources are far more copious and reliable, the atomising, data-collecting, anti-hypothesis approach obtains, and one now speaks of a range of Judaisms — Temple-Cult, Scriptural, Extra-Scriptural, Apocalyptic — rather reminiscent of the multiplication of sources for the Documentary Hypothesis, that is, the J, E, P and D and on-through-the-alphabet further strands of the Pentateuch. What began as a dissection ends as a shambles.

We would offer that the impasse could perhaps be overcome if we brought to bear upon the Scriptures the methodology of the Mythologist,[2] for it is, we maintain, the Patterns and Symbolisms of myth that the Bible has preserved at the expense of a more straightforward record. But these have their own laws and logic, which enable us to track and correlate them with the purely historical framework already put in place by Archaeology and Philology. It is worth remarking that Bible criticism went from viewing the material as Holy Writ to viewing it as History without ever stopping to consider it as myth. It is as though there were an unconscious refusal to consider the Bible as true in any but literal ways.

The Ugaritic Literature

Early in the 20th century the library of the Canaanite city of Ugarit was unearthed and deciphered, providing epoch-making insights into

---

2. We prefer this to the well entrenched but misleading term Historian of Religion.

the mythology of Israel's first high culture.³ Now the migrant Aramean population group whose adventures are abbreviated into the tales of the patriarchs had settled in Canaan by about the middle of the Bronze Age (c. 1900 BC); some of these went down to Egypt during the Hyksos period (c. 1750-1550 BC) and returned at the Exodus (c. 1250 BC). Thus, by the time David wrote his psalms, his people had been speaking Hebrew (a dialect of Canaanite) for about 1,000 years. The influence of Canaanite myth and culture was inevitably profound.

A variety of interpretations have been offered for the Baal cycle, the most mythological of the Ugaritic texts and that which has the most echoes in the Bible, but the most generally useful, we feel, were those offered by Gaster in *Thespis*. Despite some "Myth and Ritual" school excesses, the work remains quite sound: after all, an epic which centers on the struggles between the rain-god and the drought-god is by anyone's standards a parade example of Year-Cycle mythology. But Gaster has fallen far from favor today, and the most recent development has been a tendency to concentrate on "large ideas," e.g., Kingship, Cosmogony, Life vs. Death; that is, themes that almost have more affinity with belles lettres.⁴

Canaanite Influence on the Bible

While pure Ugaritic studies have thus narrowed in on themselves in the direction of literary appreciation, Biblical scholars have essentially treated the Canaanite input as another textual strand. None of the clear parallels have gone unnoticed, but there has been a general lack of success in showing how the Canaanite material combined and harmonized with other levels of text. It is however generally agreed that at least 20 percent of the Canaanite parallels cannot be ignored — though the other equally visible 80 percent which these indicate have been wilfully ignored.

Our end cannot be compassed without questioning some of the most influential studies, taking as our touchstone the very central ques-

---

3. See Coogan, *Stories from Ancient Canaan,* for the most readable version of the texts and a precis of the scholarship.
4. These are usefully surveyed by Mark S. Smith in "Interpreting the Baal Cycle, " *Ugarit Forschungen* 18, 1986, pp. 313-39).

tion of the relation of the Canaanite sky-god El to the Hebrew Yahweh with whom he is everywhere equated in the Bible. F. Cross' programmatic *Canaanite Myth and Hebrew Epic* (1971), approaching the subject from the *traditionsgeschichtliche* side, made (chs. 1-2) the Canaanite El a patriarchal lord who ruled the squabbling gods of his household like a bedouin chieftain. This prestigious god-type, he asserts, is the model for all the gods of the patriarchs — even Yahweh (ch. 3) is only one of his epithets.

But, we would ask, since Canaanite El is, as is typical for sky-gods (e.g., Greek Ouranos, Sumerian Anu) a weak figure —a *deus otiosus* — how is it this the feeble figure comes to be made, against type, the Almighty God of the Bible?

While some have supported and developed Cross' positions (e.g., Mark S. Smith's *The Early History of God, Yahweh and the Other Deities in Ancient Israel*, Harper & Row 1990), they have done so without explaining how Yahweh was extorted from El. The point may well be moot, since this party has been generally bypassed by a far more radical trend in Bible scholarship, which applies even more sterilizing scepticism to the material, questioning whether the Ugaritic texts, which may have as much as two hundred years and two hundred miles between them and the Psalms, can be used at all to clarify the Bible. These critics have made of the Biblical record a *pointillist* mural of "verifiable facts" so diffuse that no real picture emerges.[5] Thus the silence of the *Anchor Bible Dictionary*.

We shall not further pursue the survey of recent literature, since these references suffice to make our point: all have attempted to deduce the relation of the Canaanite material to the Bible and Hebrew religion using purely the techniques of the philologist, the historian and the archaeologist. But because of the unique editorial forces at work in the Bible, which altered and interwove the various strands of text for purposes that were openly hostile to what we would consider scientific his-

---

5. For surveys of this trend see Herbert Niehr, "The Rise of YHWH in Judahist and Israelite Religion: Methodological and Religio-Historical Aspects," in *The Triumph of Elohim, from Yahwism to Judaism*, Ed. Edelman, Eerdmans, Michigan, 1996; also the introduction to Rainer Albertz, *A History of Israelite Religion in the Old Testament Period*, Westminster, Louisville KY, 1994.

tory, these tools cannot alone decipher the material.

We are not dealing with a historical record that includes accounts of divine intervention, such as we find in Livy or Herodotus, but an *Historia Sacra* which includes accounts of human intervention. Thus an understanding of how religious Symbolisms determine the shape of mythic histories is essential to a clear understanding of the material. But the last 50 years of scholarship has, on the contrary, judged a pointedly theological record on its merits as history (which are uneven) and this poor showing as a historical record was in turn held against its validity as a religious one. But, we assert, the changing forms of religious Symbolisms provide an historical evidence as datable and useful as that provided by changing verbal forms.

This requires the recognition that there are in all religions recurrent Symbolisms, which reliably reappear with defined constellations of ideas and images, whose endurance cannot be explained by literary or artistic tradition alone, and which are suceptible to confirmation by detailed cross-cultural parallels.

The methodology which is here advocated is in essence the Archetypalism originally developed by Mircea Eliade. There have of course been certain modifications: Eliade himself at times inclined to a dubiously evolutionary view of History of Religion, (e.g., his assessment of Christianity at the end of *The Eternal Return*). Further, Eliade only applied his methodology to Archaic Cultures; he never succeeded in using it to understand Scriptural religion (his analyses of Judaism, Islam, &c. in his *A History of Religious Ideas* are mere summaries of scholarly received opinion, while his book on alchemy never integrated his analysis of the symbols with their articulated meaning in the texts.)

Accordingly, it is a further, even a post-Eliadeian stage of Mythologic we are applying here, and so we are at a distinct disadvantage as regards secondary literature: there are no pertinent works on the Hebrew Bible by Eliade or his successors, nor have Biblical scholars considered approaching the material from our perspective.

What we hope to show here is that while the Canaanite material provided the symbolic vocabulary for the lion's share of Hebrew Theology —this material *was used very selectively, and what was select-*

ed underwent a process of abstraction and refinement in accord with a definite agenda (— an alteration which is only visible to one who knows that is typical for a given Symbolism.) In short, our thesis is that a prior religious conception seems to underlie all the principal theological symbols and thinking of the Bible for the roughly 1,000 years of its composition. If this point can be proven, we may then enquire, with greater hopes of success, what was that underlying agenda — which may have been the original Mosaic conception of God. Reasoning back from the vast dossier of effects to the all-too-delphically attested cause, we may attain a glimpse, clearer than heretofore possible, of what Moses meant.

But if an approach to Moses' thought is too much to claim at present, this is not the case as regards the Prophets. To date, the study of the prophetic literature has concentrated on interpreting their *explicit and abstract statements* —about social justice, humility, faith, &c. *This is not however how the main thrust of their message was expressed.* During the period of the Hebrew Bible's composition there was no abstract vocabulary even for things like colors, and so, perforce, subtle or complex ideas had to be expressed in story and figurative language. Attempts to interpret the Prophets as theology, without taking into account their mythology, were productive only of superficial pieties, and these have rightly been rejected by the sceptical scholarship of the 20th century. But we may now be in a position to hear the message of the prophets more distinctly.

Here then we shall undertake to play Oedipus to such riddles as why Adam went naked, and whether there are hills in Paradise, how weary old Father El became Almighty God, why Creation begins and ends with a *Day.*. We may come to know in what garden grew, and what hand plucked the famous grapes of wrath. Puzzling questions to be sure, but not beyond all conjecture.

Historical Overview

We shall here present a precis of Israel's religious history, for the sake of giving the non-specialist reader a summary of the view taken by modern scholarship. This knowledge has not had a particularly wide circulation since, on the one hand, religious scholars tend to present the facts in a way calculated to minimize their impact, and secular scholars are often so concerned to engage the rest of the scholarly literature that their findings are effectively buried beyond the sounding of the non-specialist.

The Exodus and "Conquest"

There was of course no "conquest" of Canaan, but rather a gradual synthesis of the Hebrew migrants with the indigenous population. The Book of Joshua must be seen for what it is, a national epic, like Livy's *History of Rome:* it is very important at a certain stage in a nation's growth to imagine that they were once great bullies.

During this period of fusion, the "time of the Judges," (c. 1250-1000 BC,) Mosaic Yahwism struggled with two rivals: its own people's background of nomadic clan religion, and Canaanite polytheism, the former of which it absorbed, and the latter as well though with considerable indigestion. The clan gods, such as those of Abraham, Isaac and Jacob, were simply and easily incorporated, made early theophanies of Yahweh; the idea of a "god of the fathers," along with the concept of divine covenant, are probably the most essential contributions of patriarchal to Israelite religion.

The Kingdom

Canaanite religion contributed Jerusalem as a cult-capital, and the entire structure of the Temple and its traditions of sacrifice &c. Prophecy is of course a universal phenomenon, but there is no doubt that the formal cultic role of prophets was taken over from the Canaanites —this is shown by the identical language used to describe the function and activities of Yahwist and Canaanite prophets. If further confirmation is needed, the quantity of Canaanite myth employed by the prophets, the subject of this volume, should supply it.

In reading the Kingdom period as that in which the most wholesale adoptions from the Canaanites took place, we follow the Biblical account itself. Traditional and even modern scholarship has tended to skew the facts in order to maintain the "purity" of the prophets. In the sense in which this purity is intended, nothing of the kind is even contemplated until after the Exile.

It was also the Kingdom period when the patriarchal narratives were first recast (J text) into a continuous national history; Yahweh likewise was then nationalized into a strategic possession and instrument of policy.

After the Exile

The Babylonian Exile (587 BC) which removed the Hebrews from their land for 70 years, brought about the reformulation of the Hebrews' religion roughly along the lines suggested by the Prophets, as something very close to what we now call Judaism. This abstract idea of what the religion of the Hebrews should be, and the dream of a glorious restoration if they were loyal to it, held the people together through the Exile.

This was also the time (6th and 5th centuries) when the great Prophets (especially Deutero-Isaiah) presented their critique of the royal and cultic national religion, contemporary with the Upanishads that reinterpreted Vedic religion, as Confucius and Lao Tzu did Chinese tradition, and Greek Philosophy did Homeric religion. In the prophets we find a turning from mythological henotheism to more abstract theological monotheism, and a shifting of emphasis from cultic and national to individual and universal religious experience. It is traditional to interpret this purely as the salutary response to national catastrophe, but this depends on the impossible assertion that there was no Greek influence on the Hebrews. When we consider that the Greeks were, by the time of the Exile, far from unknown in the eastern Mediterranean, that they had by the 5th century turned back the Persian advance, and by the fourth century come to rule Palestine, it seems incredible that the Hannukah story of "no Hellenic influence" should still be believed — particularly since the Hannukah story itself only survives in a Greek translation! But these are points we shall attempt to sustain in the second volume of this work.

Now as soon as the Persian conquest of Babylon brought the exiles back (5th c. BC), and it became possible to *implement* the Yahwist paradise everyone had been so misty-eyed about, the people promptly split into two factions, the details of whose sordid squabbles are the sum of Jewish history until the land was lost in the 1st c. AD.

On the one hand you had the priestly class, heritors of the kingdom's aristocratic traditions, a cynical, worldly and propertied group who actually did hold power — under the Persians, under the Greeks (after Alexander's conquest c. 332 BC,) and under the Romans (1st c. BC — 1st c. AD.) On the other hand you had the religious purists who as early as Ezra (c. 458 BC) had formulated the Pentateuch, invoking the old nomadic concept of the Covenant (in desuetude for 500 years, since the foundation of the kingdom) to establish their concept of religious law as a contract with God, binding upon the entire people.

A rather distorted view of the post-exilic period, as one of great theocratic rigor, is given by books such as Deuteronomy. These documents are written by the out-of-power religious zealots, who describe (and project onto the past) their notion of the ideal state. Their Torah is then in many ways comparable Plato's (nearly contemporary) *Republic*, and is no more trustworthy as a guide to political reality.

The zealots in question would develop into the Pharisees, and finally the Rabbis. The priestly faction were the ancestors of the Saducees. (This genealogy of the Pharisees and Saducees is not at present accepted: but then, neither is any other. Our evidence will be presented in volume two.)

This then is the outline without the usual pieties, and will, we hope, be of some use in understanding our description of this or that text as Early, Kingdom Period, or Late.

The Psalter[6]

A further note is due with regard to the Psalter, which has till now been interpreted by scholarship only thematically, not historically. We believe it is possible, however, on the basis of internal evidence, to block in the principal dates for the book's main divisions and observe the development of the Psalms as both a spiritual and political entity — which of course parallels the historical precis above. (There are a few exceptions to the historical outline we will give, e.g., psalms 1 and 2 which were inserted at a later date as an introduction to the book. We, for the sake of clarity and concision, will not dwell on these but present the overall model with the understanding that it is slightly idealized.)

The Davidic Psalter

First come the "Psalms of David," (1-41) in which nearly all are ascribed to him, in which the name Yahweh is used for God exclusively, and in which the text is more corrupt than in any other stratum.

There is nothing to suggest a single author, and the conviction that this or that particular psalm is by the historical David is at best a matter of taste. (I personally think these are an anthology of psalms, some by David but most composed during the period of the Judges and collect-

---

6. The broad premises of the historical reading I propose are generally accepted. It is agreed that 3-41 are the oldest, that the book as a whole was completed by the fourth century. The explicitly royal and national content of the central sections are indisputable, as is the post-exilic character of much of the last collection. A breakdown by time and content such as I have done is a novelty, owing to the inordinate influence of H. Gunkel and J. Begrich's *Einleitung in die Psalmen,* (Goettingen: Vanderhoeck & Ruprecht, 1933), which pioneered the approach of examining the psalms in the context of their cultic use. Though this has been an extraordinarily profitable way of approaching much of the material, it has become a vice, and modern psalm scholarship has too far abandoned consideration of historical development.

We have here and throughout the book used the translation in the Jewish Publication Society's *Tanach,* praiseworthy for its traditional Jewish reluctance to alter or amend the text. No more painfully faithful translation is available in

ed, like the love songs in Solomon's anthology, sometime during the royal period.) Still, these psalms express a consistent world-view. The following synopsis, though very far from exhausting the themes in the "Davidic" Psalter, addresses the central ones, those that form the underlying assumptions of all of them, and suffice to establish a general dating. (The examples are chosen at random as virtually every Davidic psalm illustrates some part of this paradigm.)

The poet always speaks as an individual, personally confronting God:

> Give ear to my speech, O Lord, consider my utterance.(5:1)

> I turned to the Lord and he answered me... (34:)

He expects a morally good existence to be rewarded with success and happiness:

> Whoever fears the Lord...
> He shall live a happy life and his children shall inherit the land." (25: 12-13)

> Trust in the Lord, and do good, abide in the land and remain loyal;
> seek the favor of the Lord and he will grant you the desires of your heart. (37: 3)

English. As our own rendering would necessarily appear tendentious, this one seemed preferable. We have however altered it here and there, since even this text is occasionally fudged where the editors felt some expression was inconsistent with piety.

The method of transcription for Hebrew words is our own — employing the equivalents most accessible to English orthography and pronunciation. A more rigorous transcription would be legible only to persons who already know Hebrew. The Hebrew speaker will be able to correct back from our spelling to the proper pronunciation without difficulty. It seemed more important for the present work to provide transcriptions which, if imperfect, provided the non-specialist with usable and identifiable approximations.

Contrariwise, a wicked life will be punished:

> Pay them according to their deeds, their malicious acts...(28: 4)

> For evil men will be cut off... (37: 9)

When this equation fails, the author usually blames his own knowing or unknowing faults:

> Who can be aware of errors? Clear me of unperceived guilt.
> and from willful sins keep your servant..." (19: 13-14)

> For night and day your hand lay heavy on me...
> I said, I will confess my transgressions to the Lord... (32: 4-5)

Thereupon he asks God for aid, promising a public acknowledgement and praise:

> Deliver me from a lion's mouth...
> Then I will proclaim your fame to my brethren,
> praise you in the midst of the congregation. (22: 22-23)

> ...rescue my soul from their attacks,
> my precious life from the lions,
> that I may praise you in a great congregation,
> acclaim you in a mighty throng.(35: 17-18)

This simple mechanics of divine justice represents the world-view of independent men speaking to God directly and in the first person. God is a judge, but a fair one, who can be prevailed upon to stop punishment in return for repentance, and who expects public acknowledgement of favor shown. This self-reliant and fundamentally optimistic attitude is that of the anarchic period of the Judges, between the migrations into Canaan and David's reign (1006-966.) Other reasons for the pre-kingdom dating include the lack of mention of the Temple, want of royal, collective or geographical reference that would indicate consciousness of kingdom, and the character of the dangers mentioned

— almost always ambush rather than battle (the enemy "lies in wait" or "digs a pit".)

Together these produce an image of Israel as a loose federation of tribes rather than a state. To this might be added the kind of honor typically shown God — public praise. A god so honored is more like a Bedouin chieftain jealous of his reputation and status than the later more monarchical God who demands tribute brought to his palace-like Temple.

The Royal Psalter

The next large section, psalms 42-89 constitutes the Royal Psalter, and reflects the period from the kingdom's consolidation under David (c. 1,000) to the Exile (587). This collection is marked by the overwhelming preponderance of the divine name Elohim in place of Yahweh, references to the Temple, and a significantly less corrupt text.

Other indications of general date are the topical psalms — 45, a royal wedding song, 46-48 which describe victory over the Assyrians (Sennacherib's withdrawal in 701?), and those referring to the start of the Babylonian Exile. General references to bordering countries complete the impression of international rivalry.

The mechanics of divine justice which operated in the Davidic Psalter are here changing in both emphasis and content. The authors now frequently speak in the first person plural, for the nation — these psalms are more in the character of national anthems. The wicked are now primarily Israel's collective enemies.

In keeping with the re-imagining of the Psalms' symbolic universe in national rather than personal terms, the unhappy awareness of one's faults that leads to repentance has been replaced by social discontent, again described on a civic rather than a personal scale:

> For I see lawlessness and strife in the city.
> Day and night they make their rounds on its walls,
>   evil and mischief are inside it.
> Malice is within it, fraud and deceit never leave its square.
>   (55: 10-12.)

And in place of public praise the offering of sacrifice at the Temple has become the preferred style of piety. It would be easy enough to deplore the changes in viewpoint enumerated above, but the failings entailed have been adequately enumerated by the prophets. It is more to the point to attempt an understanding of the excitement and intoxication these shifts brought, for they were at the time of their writing the "cutting edge," and it would take an accomplished sourpuss to stand aloof from enjoyment of the phenomenon as a whole —

We have here the religious consciousness of an aristocratic national power, steeped in the literary traditions of Canaan, Egypt and Iraq, celebrating their god with all the magnificence of Ancient Near Eastern taste. It seemed that the world's center had been re-established at Jerusalem, and in keeping with this high ontological status Mount Zion was imaginatively equipped with rivers (46:5), like those of Paradise, for it was now the fountain of life itself, archetypally signified by pure and saltless "living waters." In a more literary vein it was equated with Mt. Tsaphon, the Canaanite Olympus (48: 2-3). The god who dwelt here was the entire momentum of Reality, and ready to roar forward with his people in battle when the ram's-horn trumpets squealed and blared (47: 6). Imagine the grandeur of Rome or the glory of Athens raised to the level of magic power and religious significance, and you can begin to appreciate what it meant to sing these psalms in Jerusalem.

The last part of the Royal Psalter, 73-89, refers to the Exile, and involves a national repentance. Here for the first time in the Psalter the epic history of Israel is agonizingly reviewed to reveal the idolatrous tendencies that led to the Exile. But the questions posed by the Temple's destruction in 587, which seemed the equivalent of unmaking the world, were too huge and dire a theme for mere psalmistry. Accordingly the Book of Lamentations was composed, in psalm and acrostic form, quoting freely and largely from psalms 73-89. (I assume this was the case because the same tropes appear in Lamentations in more polished form.)

It should be noted that the content of this section is not completely homogenous, and a few of the compositions could well be placed, for content, among those of the Davidic Psalter.

The Priestly Psalter

This section (90-150) is principally characterized by joy. Evidently composed after the return from Babylon, it speaks for a people who felt vindicated on a cosmic scale. The return from Exile had taken place in the intellectual context of prophecy (whose implications were now generally accepted) and eschatology (whose events were immediately expected). The Messianic age was anticipated at every moment, and this accounts for the extraordinary optimism of many of these compositions.

In a development of the national and geographical view of the Royal Psalter, we find numerous psalms declaring that God will be praised by the whole earth. We are here at the very moment where Solomonic imperialism is turning into religious universalism. It is not however quite there, and an aristocratic patriotism prevails.

During the Exile the prophets had been developing a new and powerful vision of reality, involving heavy eschatology and an emphasis on morality over cultic practice that could border on the dualistic — a separation and antagonistic revaluation of spirit and matter. Ezra and Nehemiah present an adaptation of this concept on the level of popular piety and religious teaching. Nonetheless, the priestly class that ruled Judah after the exile, under the Persians, abandoned these ideals. These priests imagined for themselves a glory more imperial than celestial. By the Greek period which succeeds, they're like so many petty princes of the time, hellenised "modernists" with a self-serving commitment to the traditions that were guarantees of their privileges.

So although there is ample evidence of Prophecy's literary influence here — the near-apocalyptic praises of Jerusalem recovered — "the capital city of mankind, every human's home," the psalms are still a national and noble literature, proud of its own cosmopolitan traditions, now producing a few blossoms of what will be the final flowering of classical Hebrew *belles lettres*.

One of the most (to us) congenial points of the late Psalter's priestly worldview was its conservative adherence to the old Monotheist view of death, a philosophical vision which perhaps originally defined itself against Egypt's chthonic faith. This was attested from the earliest, as in:

> For there is no praise of you among the dead,
>   in Sheol who can acclaim you? (6: 6)

but the ultimate in this line are these ironical queries from the late Royal Psalter (and never contradicted by any succeeding psalm):

> Do you work wonders for the dead?
> Do the shades rise to praise you?
> Is your faithful care recounted in the grave,
> you constancy in the place of perdition?
> Are your wonders made known in the netherworld,
> your benificent deeds in the land of oblivion? (88: 11-13)

This viewpoint, that of the Sadducees, though reversed by the theology of Rabbinic Judaism, has never been effaced, and remains in the modern Jewish soul as an undercurrent of wry skepticism.

Chapter One

El

The Biblical El who is master of time, (in the Hebrew as in the Ugaritic phrase "father of years,") is very far from being a crude coopting of the Canaanite deity. That does occasionally take place, as in

> 2) The heavens declare the glory of El,
> the sky proclaims his handiwork.
> 3) Day utters (El's praises) to (the following) day,
>   night speaks out (El's praises) to (the following) night,
>   (i.e. each succeeding day and night are creations that
>   should inspire one to praise El).
> 4) There is no utterance, there are no words (said),
> they (day and night) speak (this praise of El) soundlessly.
> 5) Their order (i.e., the alternation of day and night) extends
>   across the whole earth,
> their message (of El's praise) to the edges of the world.
> He placed in the heavens a tent for Shamash (the sun-god),
> 6) who is like a groom coming forth from the chamber,
>   like a hero, eager to run his race.
> 7) His rising-place is at one end of heaven,
> and his circuit reaches the other;
> nothing escapes his heat. (PS. 19: 2-7)[7]

But this is an early psalm and a notable exception. Always the Hebrew tries to sift out from a Canaanite myth not the most striking and literary image but the one best suited to symbolize certain moral and philosoph-

---

7. This is a notoriously difficult psalm to translate — as in a chorus from Aeschylus, the language is exceedingly elliptical. Thus I have added glosses as necessary to point out the most plausible sense —though no interpretation of this text will be undisputed.

ical notions. To put it more simply, Hebrew culture seems to draw on Canaanite (and other Near Eastern mythologies) as a source of *ideograms*.

The unique prominence of the sky-god motif in Hebrew mythology is apparent on the most casual perusal of the texts. The Canaanite sky-god El was taken on as synonymous with the God of Moses, an identification accepted as early as our records go, and never challenged even by the prophets. This is entirely understandable: implicit in the sky are concepts such as loftiness, power, transcendence, radiance, omniscience and totality. The sky *sees all*, and, as Eliade explains, "...for primitive man...comprehension and awareness are, and remain, epiphanies of power, of sacred force. The one who sees and knows all can *do* and *is* everything."[8] Thus the sky-god's mere awareness of things brings them into being, and so he is effortlessly and implicitly the Creator. On these terms the sky-god is an entirely accurate if rather florid translation into symbol of the Monotheist idea.

The Hebrew descriptions of El exhibit all the standard features of the sky-god as described by Eliade (*Traité*: 11-35.) To summarize his treatment, the sky-god is a type found everywhere and universally conceived as creator of the universe, rain-giving guarantor of the earth's fertility, infinitely wise and prescient, and founder of the group's laws and rituals during his brief visit to the earth. The pertinence of this description to the God of the Hebrews is writ so large across the Bible that "he who runs may read."

The sky-god is also, typically, a *marginal* figure.

In the sources which are geographically the most pertinent to our inquiry we find El the Canaanite and Anu the Mesopotamian sky-god to be deities so bounded in importance that their descriptions are few and brief. What is stated of them concentrates on their uselessness. We see this most dramatically in the Ugaritic texts, where El is threatened with physical violence by his daughter Anat.

And the Virgin Anat replied:

"My father, El the Bull, will answer me,
   he'll answer me...or else

---

8. Eliade, *Traité:* 17

> I'll push him to the ground like a lamb,
> I'll make his gray hair run with blood,
>> his gray beard with gore,
> unless he gives Baal a house like the other gods'
>> and courts like Asherah's sons'."[9]

— a threat followed by El's prompt and enthusiastic acquiescence. Clearly a god who can be so managed is far from being at the top of the divine hierarchy.

Throughout the Ugaritic poems the adjectives applied to El are "merciful, compassionate," which mean not only that he does only good but that he does not punish, i.e., is ineffectual or at least can safely be ignored. This is not only an inference from the fragmentary Ugaritic epics, but the generally attested case: the sky-god is ordinarily a *deus otiosus* honored with *precisely these* pacific and equivocal titles of "Merciful, Compassionate."[10] What is striking in the case of the Hebrew El is that these very qualities become active — prestigious rather than pitiable.

The eternal peril for the (anomalously) preeminent sky-god is that he is universally regarded as the founder of laws and norms, the source of justice, and is at the same time (if he have totality and omnipotence) the author of all that occurs. Hence the world's injustice seems to accuse the sky-god of impotence, of having become a *deus otiosus*. This may well suffice to explain the ordinary marginalisation of the sky-god.

This very question comes up in regard to El in *Job*, where one of the friends upbraids:

> 13) ...What can El know?
> Can he govern through the dense cloud?
> 14) The clouds screen him so he cannot see (down to earth)
> as he moves about the circuit of heaven. (JOB 22: 13-14;)

But despite the post-exilic devaluation of the sky-god which is here seriously contemplated —and powerfully expressed —it was not a position seriously taken up. For roughly the same time period offers new and

---

9. Coogan, *Stories,* p. 95 = ANET p. 137, E.
10. Eliade, *Traité,* 14.

dramatic exaltation of the El figure in these three late psalms (from probably the 4th-3rd centuries BC) which give an overview of the positive sky-god attributes in their fullest development.

Here the sky-god is a type of *superior and paternal goodwill:*

> 11) For as the heavens are high above the earth,
>   so great is his steadfast love toward those who fear him.
>   (PS. 103: 11)

Elsewhere in the late Psalter the sky-god symbolizes *equality and evenhandedness:*

> 5) Who is like Yahweh our God,
> who, enthroned on high,
> 6) sees what is below,
> in heaven and on earth.
> 7) He raises the poor from the dust,
> lifts up the needy from the refuse heap... (PS. 113: 5-7)

Finally the sky, which is above and has an overview of all also represents *transcendence and omniscience:*

> 9) If I take wing with the dawn
> to come to rest on the western horizon,
> 10) even there your hand will be guiding me,
> your right hand will be holding me fast.
> 11) If I say, "Surely darkness will conceal me,
> night will provide me with cover,"
> 12) darkness is not dark for you:
> night is light as day,
> darkness and light are the same (for you).
> (Ps. 139: 9-12 and cf. IS. 24: 4-5; 55: 8-9)

A consequence of the sky-god's aggrandizement was the development of that which is the most natural and immediate symbol of his influence —the Day.

Now the Hebrew conception of sacred time is strikingly different from that operant in Egypt, Canaan and Iraq. For these nations it was the agricultural yearly cycle which provided the structure of being, while for the Hebrews, with their emphasis on the sky-god (rather than the deities of weather and agriculture,) it was not the year but the day. That the day is the most essential structural unit of creation is evident from the Genesis Chapter One (Deuteronomic text, 3rd century BC) account itself, where *the day is the basic measure of divine activity.*

Indeed, it would seem plausible that at some point the Creation was held to be an action realized in a single day. Something like this seems suggested by the earlier (J-Text, c. 1000 BC) account, indeed the phrase occurs:

> 4) This is the origin of sky and earth, how they were created *in the day that God made them.* 5) There weren't yet any plants or grass in earth's fields because God had not caused it to rain upon the earth and there didn't exist any humans to till the ground. 6) Then a mist rose up from the earth
> and watered the whole surface of the ground. (GEN. 2: 4-6)

The creation takes place "in the day," and the mist that rises from the ground to water the barren earth might be read as the first morning mist — that initial morning brought everything into being just as all succeeding mornings bring the world into view.

In both accounts then, the J text (written in Solomon's time) and the Deuteronomic text (some seven hundred years later), the day is the original radiating forth of the sky-god's power. By implication Morning is the original condition of things, and every dawn constitutes a symbolic recovery the first day of creation — in a sense every day is New Year's Day, the momentous recommencement of the cycle, with all life's time-sick energies restored. This is the concept which we find in the very center of the Hebrew soul's most anguished cry for renewal — the Book of Lamentations:

> 22) The kindness of Yahweh has not ended,
> his mercies are not spent.

> 23) They *are renewed every morning*—
> ample is your grace! (LAM. 3: 22-23)

The day is described not only as theophany but as kratophany (revelation of God's power): it is the image of rescue from one's enemies, either achieved:

> 24) This is the day that Yahweh has made —
> let us exult and rejoice on it! (PS. 118)

or anticipated:

> 6) I am more eager for Yahweh
> than watchmen for the morning (PS. 130)

The Day-as-Kratophany is what makes God the master of time, the "God of History," and so, in utmost extension of this attribute, Lord of the Day of Judgement.

In Isaiah 2: 2 the abrogation of the previous world order is called the "end of days," *aharit hayamim*. This is the end or ordinary time, of mere days, which God's previous creative acts in Time brought about.

And this "end of days" introduces a new dispensation, a new Day, which is envisioned as pure show of force.

> Yahweh, whose army is the night sky's luminaries (*tsevaoth*),
> is bringing his day against (*al*)

all the high and heaven-affronting things of the natural, artificial and moral landscape — mountains, towers and human pride (IS. 2: 19-21).

The power which flattens these prominences is a kind of light, a heavy radiance that people hide in caves to escape (IS. 2: 19-21). The leveling of the terrain is not attributed to God's stamping foot, his shaping hands or his terrifying thunder — which melts mountains in the psalms — the only description of what is meant by this day is in terms of its height and splendor (*hadar, gaon*), and its terror (*pahad*). We are presented then with the sky-god's classic attributes of luminosity, loftiness, totality and awesomeness, meticulously maintained. The day symbolism is not merely the garment, but the basis of Isaiah's vision. *Gloria diei, gloria Dei.*

This is a key to understanding, and indeed to identifying the first Isaiah's writings. In the light of his vision of the Day, human pride and loftiness which *affront the heavens* are the essence of sin. Only the sky-god is exalted. To ignore his demand for the observance of the moral laws (which the sky-god archetypally establishes) is to *deny his light,* or, as Isaiah says, "they make darkness light and light darkness (IS. 5: 20). In short, the day sky is the face of God.

We find the day concept still at center stage even at the weary and disillusioned low ebb of archaic Hebrew religiosity, in Ecclesiastes (3rd century BC), where the whole repetitive, pointless and ineffectual round of human activities presided over by a touchy and unhelpful God is described with relentless repetition as what happens "under the sun." The day is used here more as a symbol of the ephemeral than the sacral character of existence, an acid refrain intoned at the expense of the most venerable Hebrew conception of sacred time. But this text, like the Deus Otiosus passage in Job, represents not a new direction in Hebrew piety but a dead end. For the concept of the Day is far from having exhausted its creative content. At roughly the same period all time was being made drastically subordinate to it:

> 4) For in your sight a thousand years
> are like yesterday that has passed,
> like a watch in the night. (PS. 90)

All that will ever occur is a single and simple manifestation of El — a day. Here the sky-god has become once more the vehicle of the Monotheistic concept in all its exhilarating purity — God is all that happens. As Isaiah has it, "Since the day was, I am He." (IS. 43: 15).

The Canaanite conception of El, as attested in Psalm 19, a highly mythological figure who directs night and day like members of a household, was, as we have seen, made, against type, an active figure and developed in the direction of his more abstract qualities, that is to say, his content. The Day symbolism which grew up alongside the more theological and less mythological El was, we believe, in itself a step in the direction of philosophical and moral abstraction. For by Second Isaiah God is already well on the way *to being conceived of as light.*[11]

If we have in some measure sharpened the reader's appreciation of how El was transformed by the genius of the Hebrews, we are yet far from our goal. For to make even these major modifications to a god-form already compatible with Yahweh does not, perhaps, require all the poetic power of an Isaiah. A real challenge however —as the prophets well realized —was presented when El's clear sky was overcast by the clouds of Baal. But an analysis of that phenomenon could not be undertaken so long as the heavens of El were accepted as a "given" and unexamined.

---

11. The Hebrew concept of holiness is, we hold, tributary to the day-concept. The word for Holy *qadosh,* is usually taken to mean "set apart," (i.e., from the profane or the ordinary) but this depends on the assumption that we have here to do with the linguistically improbable expansion of the root *qd* which, at the beginning of other words e.g. *qedem,* may suggest some concept of separation. But in Akkadian, the only language where the root occurs independently of its Biblical use, the word *quddushu* has the primary meaning "shining, gleaming," and is used parallel to such words as *ebbu,* "pure," and *ellu,* "shining." [Ringgren, *Israelite Religion,* pp. 73-74.]

This would explain the Ugaritic use of *qudshu* for Asherah. Albright remarks that the usual translation of this word, "holy," is an odd epithet for the goddess of love as patroness of ritual prostitution. [Albright, *Archaeology,* p. 75.]

We may now solve the conundrum by taking the word to mean "bright" also in the sense of sensual splendor or pornographic glory. The concept of physical radiance is ordinarily intrinsic to the love goddess: Hathor, with whom Asherah was conflated in Egypt, is ordinarily give the epithet "golden" *(nebewet)* — as in Greece was Aphrodite (who is *chruse.*)

This would clarify Job 36: 13-14: ordinarily it is translated:

> Proud men rage against him
> and do not cry to him for help when caught in his toils;
> so they die in their prime
> like male prostitutes, worn out. (New English Bible)

The image of the old tired male whore is striking, to be sure, but in this context a trifle bizarre. If we read the *baq'deshim,* which they render

> like male prostitutes, worn out.

as

> "in the radiance (we would say, in the bloom,) of their youth"

we have a perfect parallelism of the sort which is characteristic of Hebrew poetry.

> so they die in their prime,
> in the bloom of their youth.

This reading also has the merit of acknowledging that *q'deshim* here is prefaced by *b,* "in," not *k,* "like." Also, "worn out" doesn't have to be invented and inserted.

We are of course not suggesting that *qadosh* is to be translated as "bright" in every instance: it is often used in a colorless way simply to mean sacred: but there are notable cases, such as Isaiah's famous threefold sanctification (IS. 6:3), where God is called the Lord of the hosts of the sky's luminaries *(ts'vaoth),* whose glory *(k'vodo)* fills the earth. When in such a context the term qadosh is applied to God thrice in succession *(qadosh! qadosh! qadosh!)* to recognize the undertones of "luminosity" in the word is to provide some genuine enhancement to our understanding.

Chapter Two

Baal

Storm-God and Chaos-Dragon

A battle with the Dragon of the Waters is a universal myth, describing the mastery of nature for agriculture, particularly as regards setting up earthworks and canals to protect fields from flooding by rain-swollen rivers — "dismembering" the flood. The regularity of irrigation, not the caprice of an inundation, will henceforth determine the success of the harvest. There are of course many other themes at play in these cosmogonic poems, but this seems to be the primary one.

The best quick substantiation of this theory is to examine the form the myth takes in differing levels of cultures. In this tale from the Micmac Indians of the far North East of America, a pre-agricultural, hunter-gatherer society. a bullfrog has dammed up and drunk all the water and the country is dying of thirst. The world-shaper culture-bringer divinity, Glooskap, defeats the creature thus:

> And having come to the monster, he (Glooskap) said, "Give me to drink, and that of the best, at once, thou Thing of Mud!" But the chief reviled him, and said, "Get thee hence, to find water where thou canst." Then Glooskap thrust a spear into his belly, and lo! there gushed forth a mighty river; even all the water which should have run on while in the rivulet, for he had made it into himself. And Glooskap, rising high as a giant pine, caught the chief in his hand and crumpled in his back with a mighty grip. An lo! it was the Bull-Frog. So he hurled him with contempt into the stream, to follow the current.
>
> And ever since that time the Bull-Frog's back has crumpled wrinkles in the lower part, showing the prints of Glooskap's awful squeeze.[12]

---

12. Leland, *Algonquin Legends,* "How Glooskap conquered the Great Bull-Frog" p. 118.

In the Ugaritic Baal epic, Yam (Ocean) makes a bid for cosmic dominance. Baal crushes him with his war-hammers. In a pleasing mistranslation, which Coogan follows, Baal then (amazingly) drinks him. (We give Ginsberg's correct translation in a footnote). The false reading is almost justified because in the preponderance of parallels from other (more technologically advanced) cultures, the water-dragon of chaos is dismembered after the battle for world-rule. That Baal, in contrast, is satisfied with Yam's defeat, that Yam is preserved as an integral part of Baal's world-order, is almost to say that Agricultural rain-god incorporates within himself the destructive vitality of the water-chaos monster.

> The club danced in Baal's hands,
>   like a vulture from his fingers.
> It struck Prince Sea on the shoulder,
>   Judge River between the arms.
> Sea was strong; he did not sink;
>   his joints did not shake;
>   his frame did not collapse.
> Kothar (the blacksmith of the Canaanite gods) brought
>   down two clubs,
>   and he pronounced their names:
> "As for you, your name is Chaser;
> Chaser, chase Sea,
>   chase Sea from his throne,
>   River from the seat of his dominion.
> Dance in Baal's hands,
>   like a vulture from his fingers.
> Strike Prince Sea on the skull,
>   Judge River between the eyes.
> Sea will stumble,
>   he will fall to the ground."
> And the club danced in Baal's hands,
>   like a vulture from his fingers.
> It struck Prince Sea on the skull,
>   Judge River between the eyes.
> Sea stumbled;
>   he fell to the ground;
>   his joints shook;

his frame collapsed.
Baal captured and drank Sea;
he finished off Judge River.[13]
Astarte shouted Baal's name:
"Hail, Baal the Conqueror!
   hail, Rider on the Clouds!
For Prince Sea is our captive,
   Judge River is our captive."

A more normative account of the struggle for world-rule is this violent parallel from Mesopotamia, wherein Marduk slays the chaos-sea-serpent Tiamat, and builds the universe from her corpse:

Then they met: Marduk, that cleverest of gods, and Tiamat grappled alone in single fight.
The lord shot his net to entangle Tiamat, and the pursuing tumid wind, Imhullu, came from behind and beat in her face. When the mouth gaped open to suck him down he drove Imhullu in, so that the mouth would not shut but wind raged through her belly; her carcass blown up, tumescent, she gaped — And now he shot the arrow that split the belly, that pierced the gut and cut the womb
Now that the Lord had conquered Tiamat he ended her life, he flung her down and straddled the carcass; the leader was killed, Tiamat was dead, her rout was shattered, her band dispersed.

(There follows a description of how Marduk vanquished the gods who had been Tiamat's allies.)

---

13. Coogan, Stories, pp. 88-89 = ANET 130-31: (2) III AB A, where Ginsberg has:

Baal would rend, would smash Yamm,
   would annihilate Judge Nahar.
By name Ashtoreth rebukes [him].
   "For shame, O puissant [Baal];
For our captive is Prin[ce Yamm]...

> He turned to where Tiamat lay bound, he straddled the legs and smashed her skull (for the mace was merciless), he severed the arteries and the blood streamed down the north wind to the unknown ends of the world.
>
> When the gods saw all this they laughed out loud, and they sent him presents. They sent him thankful tributes.
>
> The lord rested; he gazed at the huge body, pondering how to use it, what to create from the dead carcass. He split it apart like a cockle-shell; with the upper half he constructed the arc of sky, he pulled down the bar and set a watch on the waters, so they should never escape.[14]

This gives us a complete spectrum of attitudes towards irrigation and land-mastery — from the playful Indian tale to the sadistic Mesopotamian version; the theme is more grandiose and its content more cruel in proportion as the level of agriculture is extensive and laborious. The Canaanite tale, probably since theirs was primarily a trading society, occupies a middle position. We have discussed this Pattern at considerable length because it is one that is quite extensively drawn on and fatefully developed by the Hebrew authors who, like their Canaanite predecessors, preserve the chaos-dragon as an integral and powerful (if subordinate) part of the orderly cosmos.

There are many allusions in the Bible to the victory over the chaos-dragon, all clearly modeled on Canaanite material. The most explicit are these:

> 1) Ascribe to Yahweh, O divine beings, ascribe to Yahweh glory and strength.
> 2) Ascribe to Yahweh to glory of his name; bow down to Yahweh, majestic in holiness.
> 3) The voice of Yahweh is over the waters (of the ocean), the God of glory thunders, Yahweh, over the might waters.
> 4) The voice of Yahweh (i.e., thunder) is power; the voice of Yahweh is majesty;
> 5) the voice of Yahweh breaks cedars; Yahweh shatters the cedars of Lebanon.

---

14. Sandars, *Heaven and Hell,* pp. 90-92 = ANET p. 67: 93-106, 128-40.

> 6) he makes Lebanon skip like a calf, Sirion like a young
>   wild ox.
> 7) The voice of Yahweh (i.e., lightning) kindles flames of fire,
> 8) the voice of Yahweh convulses the wilderness of Kadesh,
> 9) the voice of Yahweh causes hinds to calve and strips
>   forests bare
> while in his temple all say "Glory!"
> 10) Yahweh sat enthroned on the Flood,
> Yahweh sits enthroned, king forever. (PS. 29: 1-10)

The prototype of this Yahweh, who discharges thunder and lightning from his mouth, and whose storming ends with his enthronement on a evidently subjugated Flood (i.e., Ocean), is clearly Baal. Another example of the myth in Hebrew adaptation is:

> 7) In my distress I called on Yahweh,
> cried out to my god, in his temple he heard my voice,
> my cry to him reached his ears.
> 8) Then the earth rocked and quaked;
> the foundations of the mountains shook, rocked by his
>   indignation;
> 9) smoke went up from his nostrils,
> from his mouth came devouring fire, live coals blazed forth
>   from him.
> 10) He bent the sky (i.e. the rain-clouds were low and heavy
>   in the heavens)
> and came down, thick cloud beneath his feet.
> 11) He mounted a cherub and flew, gliding on the wings of
>   the wind.
> 12) He made darkness his screen,
>   dark thunderheads, dense clouds of the sky were his
>   pavilion around him.
> 13) Out of the brilliance before him
>   hail and fiery coals (i.e. lightning) pierced his clouds.
> 14) Then Yahweh thundered from heaven,
>   the most high gave forth his voice — hail and fiery coals.
> 15) He let fly his shafts and scattered them, he discharged
>   lightning and routed them.
> 16) The ocean bed was exposed,

>   the foundations of the world were laid bare
>   by your mighty roaring, Yahweh,
>   at the blast of the breath of your nostrils. (PS. 18: 7-16)[15]

Here again we have Yahweh dressed in Baal's storm-god attributes, making a spectacular display of power which ends in a reference to the Ocean being routed.

These Baal-psalms are from the earliest period of Israel's history, the time of the migration into Canaan (later re-imagined as the "Conquest,") during which the Hebrews peacefully amalgamated with and adopted the more sophisticated culture of the Canaanites. Since Moses' group already spoke a Canaanite dialect (Hebrew), they made rather direct appropriations from Canaanite literature.

Still, this incorporation of Baal material is fairly superficial: no more theologically meaningful than Milton's borrowings from Graeco-Roman myth to gussy up his Christian epic. Somewhat greater significance is to be accorded the later (Kingdom period) development of Baal-Yahweh as a political and military emblem. In this context foreign powers were routinely equated with the waves of the chaos-dragon. e.g.

>   12) Ah, the roar of many peoples that roar as roars the sea,
>   the rage of nations that rage as rage the mighty waters —

---

15. The notion of the ocean covering the earth's foundations is a little more complicated than what would naturally occur to the modern reader:

> "The world was thought of (in the ancient Near East) as a self-contained structure; in Israel, it was first conceived of as bipartite (heaven-earth) and later, under Mesopotamian influence, as tripartite (heaven-earth-abyss). Heaven represents a gigantic bell-shaped dome inverted over the earth; above it are the waters of heaven and the heavenly palace of the deity, below it the stars and constellations move about. The earth is a flat surface with four corners, or, on account of the horizon, a round disc; it rests on posts or pillars. The latter are fixed in the waters of the abyss under the earth; this water feeds the springs and watercourses of the earth, until it possibly returns once more to the abyss. Within or beneath the abyss lies the realm of the dead, which is usually thought of a belonging to the third portion of the world." — Fohrer, *Israelite Religion,* p. 180.

> 13) nations raging like massive waters!
> But he shouts at them, and they flee far away,
> driven like chaff before winds in the hills,
> and like tumbleweed before a gale. (IS. 17: 12-13)

Similarly, Psalm 74 describes the destruction of the Temple in 587, and asks God to smite the Babylonians as once he did Leviathan:

> 13) ...it was you who drove back the sea with your might,
> who smashed the heads of the sea monsters *(tanniyniym al hammayiim);*
> 14) it was you who crushed the heads of Leviathan,
> who left him as food for the denizens of the desert.
> (PS. 74: 13-14)

The further examples of this political use of the Dragon-Battle motif will be given later in this chapter, for they are importantly subordinated to a larger schema. For the moment we shall confine ourselves to the remaining merely literary uses of the symbolism — those which did not form a better than decorative enhancement of the Yahweh concept. Of this sort is the allusion to the smiting of Rahab ("arrogance," an epithet for Yam/Leviathan,) in the creation account in the Book of Job:

> 10) He drew a boundary on the surface of the waters (i.e., set the horizon in place at the edges of the world-disk encircling sea),
> at the extreme where light and darkness meet (i.e., as far in every direction as light and darkness reach).
> 11) The pillars of heaven tremble, astonished at his blast (i.e., thunder).
> 12) By his power he stilled the sea, by his skill he struck down Rahab.
> 13) By his wind the heavens were calmed; his hand pierced the oblique(ly writhing) Serpent.
> 14) These are but glimpses of his rule, the mere whisper that we perceive of him. Who can absorb the thunder of his mighty deeds? (JOB 26: 10-14)

— but this is no more than to say "all this he shaped from Chaos." That this is not a meaningful reference is clear from the treatment of Leviathan in Job chapters 40-41, he is there, as in Psalm 104, merely a big beast, an instance of God's unbridled creativity, with nothing to suggest Yahweh's opponent.

Our last example of the motif is:

> ...the earth being unformed and void (i.e., scattered and shapeless debris), with darkness over the face of the waters (i.e., when there was only darkness above and the chaos-ocean *(Tehom)* below), and a wind from God *(ruah Elohim)* sweeping over the water... (GEN. 1: 2)

This is the final significant appearance of the Pattern in Scripture. The spirit, *ruah,* literally "breath" or "wind" of God hovering over the chaos-waters, *Tehom* (a word cognate with the Babylonian Tiamat), is the latest attenuated descendant of the ocean-subduing storm-god.

Tsedeq and the Sacred King

The closest Baal ever came to truly competing with Yahweh was not in these rather literary hymns, but in the royal cultus. For the Near East, the king's central role is as the representative or incarnation of the Male Agricultural deity. The parade example of this analogy between Royal and Cosmic rule is the Babylonian New Year's Festival where the king personates Marduk. The text recited on this occasion includes:

> Powerful master of the Igigi gods, exalted among the great gods,
> Lord of the world, king of the gods, divine Marduk, who establishes the plan,
> Important, elevated, exalted, superior,
> Who holds kingship, grasps lordship,
> Bright light, god Marduk, who dwells in the temple Eudul
> ...who sweeps the enemy's land,
> ...(three lines missing)...

Who ...'s heaven, heaps up earth,
Who measures the waters of the sea, cultivates the fields,
Who dwells in the temple Eudul; lord of Babylon, exalted Marduk,
Who decrees the fates of all the gods,
Who turns over the pure scepter to the king who reveres him —
(ANET p. 332 l. 222 ff.)

The king is here explicitly equated with Marduk, and so master of both the political and agricultural cosmos. Like Baal he controls sea and masters the landscape as the one "...Who measures the waters of the sea, cultivates the fields..."

In the Hebrew coronation hymns we see a rather precise parallel.[16] Presumably these were recited to explicitly equate the king's rule, renewed for another year cycle, with the original cosmic coronation of Baal/Yahweh.

1) Yahweh is king! Let the earth exult, the many islands rejoice!
2) Dense clouds are around him,
Justice and Fairness *(Tsedeq umishpat)* are the foundations of his throne.
3) Fire goes forth before him, burning up his enemies one every side.
4) His lightnings light up the world: the earth is convulsed at the sight.
5) Mountains melted like wax at the presence of Yahweh, at the presence of the Lord of the whole earth.
6) The heavens declare his just ordering of the world *(tsidqo,)* and all the people see his glory. (PS. 97: 1-6)

1) Yahweh reigneth, he is clothed with majesty;
the Lord is clothed with strength

---

16. The use of these, the "enthronement" psalms in a Hebrew New Year's Festival received its classic treatment from S. Mowinckel, *Psalmenstudien* 2, 1922, repr. Amsterdam, Verlag P Schippers 1961; and *Zum Israelitischen Neujahr und zur Deutung der Thronbesteigungspsalmen* Oslo, J. Dybwad, 1952. The material is available in translation as *The Psalms in Israel's Worship*, vol. 1, Oxford, Blackwell 1962.

> which he has fastened on like a belt,
> and (by analogy) the world also is established that it cannot
>   be shaken.
> 2) Your throne is established from of old, from eternity you
>   have existed.
> 3) The ocean sounds, o Yahweh,
>   the ocean sounds its thunder, the ocean sounds its
>   pounding.
> Above the thunder of the mighty waves,
> more majestic than the breakers of the sea,
> is Yahweh, majestic on high. (PS. 93: 1-4)

We are here very clearly dealing with the motifs of the storm-god and the rebellious chaos-ocean, but the images of lightning and flood are all but fused into a single kratophanous explosion. This uproar of fire and water, accompanied by the quaking and melting of the earth, comes very close in language and content to Moses' Song at the Sea, where God was seen as an eruption on every plane, in every element.

As the Baal-Leviathan myth dissolves into a single combustive act which we are tentatively equating with Yahweh in action, one feature of it arises in with greater clarity. This feature is the *result* of the battle: on one level this is simply establishment of the orderly cycles of the agricultural world, but these become the type and pattern of political and social harmony, the image of justice.

A number of words are used for this moral/cosmic order: *emet, chesed, mishpat* and especially *tsedeq*. Ringgren excellently observes that tsedeq, usually translated as "righteousness,"

> "...is neither exclusively nor even primarily a juristic concept. On the basis of Arabic, the original meaning of the root is something like "be right, stable, substantial." ...the nuances can be derived from the definition 'conformity to a norm.'"

As Ringgren goes on to show, in a military context *tsedeq* can mean "victory which re-asserts the world's just order." Sociologically, it means conformity with the norms of society. On the cosmic scale it is used of rainfall sent "at the proper time" *litsdaqa* (Ps. 85: 12 ff.) It is accordingly very similar to the Babylonian *mesharu* and the Egyptian *ma'at*.[17]

The idea of the king as the embodiment and guarantor of *Tsedeq* seems to have been already operant in the Canaan of Abraham's time (c. 18th century BC?). After Abraham returns from defeating Chedorlaomer and the kings, he is blessed by king Mechizedek of Salem (i.e., *melkiy-tsedeq*, "my-king-is-*Tsedeq*, of *Shalem* [=Jerusalem, cf. PS. 76:2])

Later Joshua (13th century BC) is opposed by a king of Jersualem named of *Adoni-Tsedeq (my-lord-is-Tsedeq* JOSH. 10: 1 ff.)

A late and very explicit coronation psalm makes it quite clear that the royal-priestly Tsedeq-King , no less than the capitol Jerusalem, is appropriated from the Canaanites: the enthronement text goes:

> 1) The Lord (God) said to my lord (the king):
> "Sit at my right hand
> while I make your enemies your footstool...
>
> 4) The Lord has sworn and will not back down:
> "You are a priest forever, after the manner of
> Melchizedeq."(PS. 110: 1-4)[18]

More light on the meaning of Tsedeq — as the underlying condition of existence —comes forward in these two psalms from the Kingdom period:

> 10) His help is very near those who fear him —
> he will make his radiance (sunlight?) dwell in our land.
> 11) His Generosity *(hesed)* and his Fairness *(emeth)* will be inseparable.
> God's justice *(tsedeq)* will be to effect general well-being *(shalom):*
> what's right and what's profitable will be things so closely allied they kiss.[19]
> 12) The land will bring forth in one movement grain and equity *(emeth),*

---

17. Ringgren, Israelite Religion, pp. 83-84.

18. Paul will continue the tradition by identifying Jesus with Melchizedek in HEB. 5:5-7.

19. Lit., "Faithfulness and truth meet; justice and well-being kiss."

> the skies will shine down light on a world filled with Justice *(tsedeq.)*[20]
> 13) Yahweh also bestows his Goodness (i.e., all good things,) and our land shall yield her produce. (PS. 85: 10-13)

A clear description of *Tsedeq* as what the king maintains in the land all year long is:

> 1) O Yahweh, endow the king with thy justice (lit. "judgements",)
> and the king's son with your righteousness *(tsidqathka)*,
> 2) that he may judge your people righteously *(bitsedeq,)* your poor justly.
> 3) The mountains shall produce well-being (i.e., bounty) for the people,
> and the hills as well,
> since the world-order is being maintained (lit. "in return for justice, *bitsidqa*).
> 4) He shall judge the poor of the people,
> he shall deliver the children of the needy,
> and shall break in pieces the oppressor.
> 5) They shall be in awe of him as long as the sun shines,
> and show him reverence while the moon lasts,
> for generation after generation.
> 6) He shall be like the rain that comes down upon the mown field:
> the showers that water the earth,
> so that in his days shall the righteous may flourish,
> and well-being abound till the moon is no more. (PS 72: 1-7)

The psalm continues to develop the idea most impressively, yet this excerpt suffices for our purpose, and indeed is the cornerstone of our case.[21] The Hebrew king, like the kings of Egypt or Babylon, guaranteed the land's increase like an incarnate agricultural god.

---

20. Lit., "Truth springs up from the earth; justice looks down from heaven."

21. Other examples might be multiplied, including the "just rainfall" *(yoreh tsedeq)* passage in Hosea (10:12).

It might reasonably be objected that we have here to do with a simple literary echo, and that the Enthronement Psalms are no more a serious piece of Paganism than Boileau's odes to Louis XIV which compared him to Apollo. But we think this level of desacralisation in poetry very unlikely in the first millenium BC, and such a minimizing of the "Sacred King" concept would leave much to be explained in the post-exilic mythology of the Messiah.

So then, despite the successful incorporation of the Baal-Leviathan mythos into a Yahweh-theophany, we can see that it was not accomplished without some struggle and much ingenuity. Much remains unassimilated after all — notably the concept of "sacred kingship." We can now perhaps better understand the Prophet Samuel's reluctance to anoint the first Hebrew King so they could "be like other nations," and the fact that none of the great prophets had particularly warm feelings for *any* of the royal houses.

But what is of most moment is that the adoption of the pagan royal concept took place for the sake of the *Tsedeq* idea, which was compatible with Yahweh, and that this was the motivation is shown by the fact that the *Tsedeq* idea survives the kingship, and even during the kingdom period all but overwhelms that institution — as in the famous Isaiah "Messiah" passage (IS. 11), where the king wears Justice *(Tsedeq)* like a sword-belt, and doesn't merely guarantee fertility but restores the world to its original paradisal condition.

The Conquest of Death

On whatever level Baal's tale operated in the royal mythology, it possessed a coherence and completeness exceeding what one could expect in mere literary allusion, and this is shown by the way it re-emerges as a positively religious structure in Apocalyptic literature.[22]

In Isaiah chapters 24-27 we have an apocalypse that is structurally an amplified echo of the Baal mythos (for which see Coogan, *Stories,* pp. 75-115), for that part of the cycle which concerns the summer months, which are, in the Middle East, a brutal and deadening outstretch of

---

22. The appendix gives the most significant passages we will deal with here in continuous, literary translation with commentary.

time, where motion seems madness under the white weight of sunlight. By the mythic account Baal, who presided over the rainy winter months, has been slain by the god of Death and Drought, Mot. Thus (in the Ugaritic Epic) Mot says:

> "I approached Baal the Conqueror,
> I put him in my mouth like a lamb,
> He was crushed like a kid in my jaws."

This declaration that the forces of Life have been defeated is immediately followed by the description:

> Sun, the gods' torch burned,
> the heavens shimmered under the sway of El's son, Death.[23]

immediately thereafter we learn the consequences of this are that "the furrows in the fields have dried."[24]

An identical blanching of the land under sky's heavy heat is described in Isaiah:

> 1) Behold,
> Yahweh will strip the earth bare
> and lay it waste
> and turn it upside down (i.e., make it the opposite of what
>   it was,)
> and scatter its inhabitants.
> 2) Layman and priest shall fare alike,
> slave and master,
> handmaid and mistress,
> buyer and seller,
> lender and borrower,
> creditor and debtor.
> 3) The earth shall be bare, bare;
> it shall be plundered, plundered;
> indeed it is Yahweh who spoke this word (and this shall surely come to pass.)

---

23. Coogan, *Stories,* p. 11 = ANET p. 140, h. I AB (ii)
24. This passage will be given below.

> 4) The earth is withered, sear;
> the world languishes, it is sear;
> the most exalted people of the earth languish
> 5) for the earth was defiled
> under its inhabitants;
> because they transgressed teachings,
> violated laws,
> broke the ancient covenant.
> 6) That is why a curse consumes the earth
> and its inhabitants pay the penalty;
> that is why earth's dwellers have burned *(haru)*
> and but few men are left. (IS. 24: 1-6)

The earth stripped bare, languishing and sear, consumed by a curse, with few survivors, and those *burned* — this is a very clear depiction of a punishing summer.

Isaiah then enumerates all that is lacking, all that fails, in a summer extended into *drought*. The new wine and oil of the autumn harvest is not produced. Summer endures illimitably in an endless August.

> 7) The new wine fails,
> the vine languishes
> and all the merry-hearted sigh.
> 8) Stilled is the clamor of revelers,
> stilled the merriment of lyres.
> 9) They shall not drink their wine with song,
> liquor tastes bitter to the drinker (i.e., it's too hot to drink,
> even if there were anything to drink).
> 10) Towns are broken, empty;
> every house is shut, none enter.
> 11) There is a crying for wine in the streets,
> the sun has set on all joy.
> The gladness of the earth is banished.
> 12) Desolation is left in the town
> and the gate is battered to ruins.
> 13) For thus shall it be among the peoples
> in the midst of the earth:
> as when the olive tree is beaten (to make the olives fall from
> the branches),

> like gleanings when the vintage is done (i.e., slim pickings).
> (IS. 24:7-13)

Habbakuk used the same Baal apocalypse as a paradigm; he wrote in the 7th-6th centuries and so his work comes about a hundred years after Isaiah's. Habbakuk's summer of drought goes:

> 16) I heard and my bowels quaked,
> my lips quivered at the sound;
> rot entered into my bone,
> I trembled where I stood.
> Yet I wait calmly for the day of distress,
> for a people to come to attack us.
> 17) Though the fig tree does not bud
> and no yeild is on the vine,
> though the olive crop has failed
> and the fields produce no grain,
> though sheep have vanished from the fold
> and no cattle are in the pen. (HA. 3: 16-18)

Very much later — c. 400 BC — Joel carries on the same tradition, and is much more explicit in his invocation of Canaanite myth (he can afford to be —it is by this time more a recondite literary reference than a competing religion).

Here the terrible summer is connected with mourning rites in the temple — which he very suggestively compares to a woman mourning for her husband (the word for which is *baal*).[25] We give the passage in full, as it functions as a commentary on the Isaiah:

> 8) Lament — like a maiden girt with sack cloth
> for the husband *(baal)* of her youth!

---

25. Mourning rites for the dead vegetation god in the Temple in mid-summer are in fact attested by Ezekiel (fl. 593-71):

> 14) Next he brought me to the entrance of the north gate of
> the House of the Lord; and there sat the women bewailing
> Tammuz. (EZ. 8: 14)

9) Offering and libation have ceased
from the House of the Lord;
the priests must mourn
who minister to the Lord.
10) The countryside is ravaged
the new wine is dried up,
the new oil has failed.
11) Farmers are dismayed
and vine-dressers wail
over wheat and barley;
for the crops of the field are lost.
12) The vine has dried up,
the fig-tree withers,
pomegranate, palm and apple —
all the trees of the field are sear
and joy has dried up
among men. (JO. 1: 8-12)

* * * * * * *

17) The seeds have shriveled
under their clods.
The granaries are desolate,
barns are in ruins,
for the new grain has failed.
18) How the beasts groan!
The herds of cattle are bewildered
because they have no pasture,
and the flocks of sheep are dazed.

19) To you, Yahweh, I call,
for fire (i.e., scorching heat) has consumed
the pastures in the wilderness,
and flame (i.e. heat) has devoured

Tammuz (a Hebraization of the Sumero-Akkadian Dumuzi) is a dying-reviving god cognate with Baal: Ezekiel, who writes this part of his visions in Babylon, is most likely using the name of the very similar and (now) local deity, instead of saying "Baal", for the sake of connecting the Israelites' sin (idolatry) more closely with their punishment (exile to Babylon).

> all the trees of the countryside.
> 20) The very beasts of the field
> cry out to you;
> for the water-courses are dried up
> and fire has consumed
> the pastures of the wilderness. (JO. 1: 17-18)

The Ugaritic epic gives us a fairly complete account of the following events: Baal is resurrected:

> In a dream of El, the Kind, the Compassionate
> in a vision of the Creator of All,
> the heavens rained down oil,
> the wadis ran with honey.
> El the Kind, the Compassionate, was glad;
> he put his feet on a stool,
> he opened his mouth and laughed;
> he raised his voice and shouted:
> "Now I can sit back and relax;
> my heart inside me can relax;
> for Baal the conqueror lives,
> the Prince, the Lord of the Earth has revived.[26]

El sends a message to the sun, asking the whereabouts of the revived Baal seen in the dream, explaining the need for Baal thus:

> "Sun, the furrows in the fields have dried,
> the furrows in El's fields have dried;
> Baal has neglected the furrows of his plowland.
> Where is Baal the Conqueror, where is the Prince, the Lord
> of the Earth?"
> And Sun, the gods' torch, replied:
> "Pour sparkling wine from its container,
> bring a garland for your relative;
> and I will look for Baal the Conqueror.[27]

---

26. Coogan, *Stories*, pp. 112-113 = ANET p. 140, h. I AB (iii-iv)
27. Coogan, *Stories*, p. 113 = ANET p. 140, h. I AB (iii-iv)

There follows a gap of some 35 lines, which would include a description of the rain-god's return. The next passage describes Baal's conquest of Death and the chaos-dragon.

Isaiah's apocalyptic summer is similarly ended by the return of a god who is greeted as the one who guarantees the agricultural cycle (and the moral economy which is an expansion of this idea), that is, who guarantees *Tsedeq*. We are shown a joyous crowd who

> "lift up their voices, exult in the majesty of the Lord"
> (IS. 24: 14)

then greet him with the phrase

> "Glory to the Righteous! *(latsaddiyq*, i. e., to the one
> Who establishes *Tsedeq)* " (IS. 24: 16)

Isaiah, seems to expand the idea by having a resurrection —visualized in national terms —

> 19) Oh, let your dead revive!
> Let corpses arise,
> awake and shout for joy,
> you who dwell in the dust!
> for your dew is like the dew on fresh growth,
> you make the land of ghosts give birth. (IS. 26: 19)

A passage in the very disordered writings of Hosea (late 8th century, contemporary with Isaiah) seems also to follow the Canaanite mythos on this point. Hosea's victorious autumn includes a resurrection which is again used to represent the political "return to life" of the nation:

> 1) Come, let us turn back to Yahweh;
> he tore, and he will heal us;
> he struck, and he will bandage us.
> 3) In two days he will return us to life,
> on the third day he will resurrect us and we shall be alive
>   before him.

> 4) Let us seek to know Yahweh:
> he will manifest as surely as will the dawn
> he will come to us like rain, like autumn rain
> that waters (read, w. Sept., *yarweh*) the earth.
> (HOS. 6: 1-3)

Judging from these passages, the Resurrection of the Dead —a shibboleth for the Pharisees and a central doctrine for the Christians is then, insofar as it is rooted in the prophetic writings, an extension of this phase of Baal's epic career. Similarly, the Egyptian Osiris was originally a myth applied only to Pharaoh, but gradually democratized to include the nobles, then the entire people. The Christian hope of resurrection may be based then in the exemplary life of an Ancient Near Eastern god-king in a more literal way than is generally supposed.

But to return to the myth. Isaiah's resurrection is also accompanied by the thunderstorms of late September: rains so vehement they seem almost to wash away the land.

> 18) ... for the sluices are opened on high (i.e., it rains)
> and the earth's foundations tremble (i.e., it thunders).
> 19) The earth is breaking, breaking;
> the earth is crumbling, crumbling;
> the earth is tottering, tottering. (IS. 24: 18-19)

Habakkuk also has God return with a storm theophany:

> 3)...his majesty covers the skies,
> his splendor fills the earth:
> 4) it is a brilliant light
> which gives off rays on every side —
> and therein his glory is enveloped (i.e., lightning).
> 5) Pestilence marches before him
> and plague comes forth at his heels.
> 6) When he stands, he makes the earth shake;
> when he glances, he makes nations tremble.
> The age-old mountains are shattered,
> the primeval hills sink low (i.e. shaken down by thunder
>   *   *   *   *

> 9) you make the earth burst into streams,
> the mountains rock at the sight of you.
> A torrent of rain comes down... (HA. 3: 3-10)

Joel follows his summer with a very similar storm theophany. Though Joel's account is assimilated to the description of an alien invasion, the figurative language follows Isaiah in all details, viz., clouds:

> 1) Blow a horn in Zion,
> sound an alarm on my holy mount!
> Let all the dwellers on earth tremble
> for the day of Yahweh has come,
> it is close!
> 2) a day of darkness and gloom,
> a day of densest cloud *(anan wa'araphel):*
> the hills are almost black, overspread
> by a vast enormous horde. (JO. 2: 1-2)

lightning:

> 3) Their vanguard is lightning *(esh)* that devours,
> their rear guard's a furious lightning bolt *(tilahet lehavah)*
> (JO. 2: 3)

and thunder:

> 10) Before them the earth trembles,
> the sky quakes;
> sun and moon are darkened
> and stars withdraw their brightness
> and Yahweh utters thunder *(Yahweh natan qolo* — lit. "gives his voice", a phrase equivalent to "thunders", cf. PS. 19: 1-9)
> at the head of his army. (JO. 2: 10-11)

The next chapter of Isaiah continues the mythological itinerary. After a few lines of rather generalized praise, we are favored with this astounding description:

> 6) The Lord of Hosts will make on this mountain
> for all the peoples
> a banquet of rich viands,
> a banquet of choice wines —
> or rich viands seasoned with marrow,
> of choice wines well refined.
> 7) And he will destroy on this mount the shroud
> that is drawn over the faces of all the peoples
> and the covering that is spread
> over all the nations:
> 8) he will destroy Death forever.
> My Lord God will wipe the tears away
> from all faces
> and will put an end to the reproach of his people[28]
> over all the earth —
> the Lord has spoken it. (IS. 25: 6-8)

The feast is merely an apocalyptic enlargement of the Middle East's ordinary autumn harvest festivities. It is worth noting that Baal's resurrection in the Ugaritic epic had :

> And Sun, the gods' torch, replied:
> "Pour sparkling wine from its container,
> bring a garland for your relative...

which seems to anticipate Isaiah's "banquet of choice wines"

Habbakuk gives a more menacing sense to the wine feast, but wine feast it certainly is:

> 15) Ah, you who make others drink to intoxication
> as you pour out your wrath,
> in order to gaze upon their nakedness!
> 16) You shall be sated with shame

---

28. This is the failure of crops, which would have been taken by the neighboring peoples as an indication that Israel had displeased its god(s). Cf. JO. 2: 19 cited immediately below.

rather than glory:
Drink in your turn and stagger!
The cup in the right hand of Yahweh
shall come around to you... (HA. 2: 15-16)

Joel concurs in following the storm immediately with an orgy of plenty: Joel has Yahweh "leave a blessing" (JO. 2: 4) — an agricultural one assimilated to a political harvest of peace:

19) In response to his people
Yahweh declared:
"I will grant you the new grain,
the new wine and the new oil,
and you will have them in abundance.
Nevermore will I let you be
a mockery among the nations (JO. 2: 19)

Joel shows the invader driven away, i.e., the autumn storms will pass, leaving in their wake the characteristic blessings of the restored agricultural order:

21) "Fear not, O soil, rejoice and be glad,
for the Lord has wrought great deeds;
22) fear not, O beast of the field,
for the pastures in the wilderness
are clothed with grass.
The trees have borne their fruit;
fig tree and vine
have yielded their wealth.
23) O children of Zion, be glad,
rejoice in Yahweh your God,
for he has given you the early rain in accord with righteousness *(litsdaqa)*,
now he makes the rain fall as formerly —
the autumn rain and the spring rain —
24) and threshing floors are piled with grain,
and vats shall overflow with new wine and oil.
(JO. 2: 21-24)

Isaiah's apocalyptic feast, with Joel as a gloss, is seen to be simply an enlargement of the harvest, but the death of Death (IS. 25: 8, quoted above) will prove to be more than a mere figure and figment for summer's end. In the Baal mythos, when Baal returns from the dead he battles Death and Chaos to restore the agricultural world order. The Ugaritic epic goes:

> Baal seized Asherah's sons;
> he struck Rabbim ("the many" *sc.* waters) on the shoulder;
> he struck the waves with his club;
> he pushed sallow Death to the ground.
> Baal returned to his royal chair,
> to his dais, the seat of his dominion.[29]

Habbakuk also slays death, in the person of the Babyonians whose eventual demise he foretells. These are explicity equated with Baal's old enemy in:

> 5) How much less than shall the defiant go unpunished,
> the treacherous, arrogant man
> who has made his maw as wide as Sheol,
> who is as insatiable as Death,
> who has harvested all the nations
> and gathered in all the peoples! (HA. 2: 5)

Clearly Habakkuk, like Isaiah with his "he will destroy Death forever" was giving us a sequentially appropriate allusion to the Canaanite myth, a point that is put beyond reasonable doubt when we note that Isaiah's echo of the Canaanite Baal's battle with Death and Rabbim (the chaos-dragon) is so precise as to include that latter deity:

---

29. Coogan, *Stories,* p. 114 = ANET p. 141, h. I AB (v) —the defeat of Death requires the completion of a defective line, but is justified by the succeeding section (vi) which includes (ANET version): "Sore afraid was Godly Mot, filled with dread was El's beloved Ghazir. Mot... [...] Baal seats him [on] his kingdom's [throne]...

> 1) In that day the Lord will punish
> with his great, cruel, mighty sword
> Leviathan, the quick and coiling serpent,
> and he will slay the Dragon of the Sea. (IS. 27:1)

Similarly, Habbakuk follows the death of Death with a Dragon Battle, actually using the old Ugaritic Epic names *Yam* and *Neharim*:

> 9) Are you wroth, Yahweh, with Neharim?
> Is your anger against Neharim,
> you rage against Yam —
> that you are driving your steeds,
> your victorious chariot?
> 9) All bared and ready is your bow,
> sworn are the rods of your word.
> You make the earth burst into streams,
> the mountains rock at the sight of you.
> A torrent of rain comes down,
> loud roars the deep,
> the sky returns the echo.
> Sun and moon stand still on high
> as your arrows fly in brightness,
> your flashing spear in brilliance.
> You tread the earth in rage,
> you trample nations in fury. (HA. 3: 8-12)

The seventh century prophet Nahum, whose works are too disordered to permit insight into his overall conception, does however quite unambiguously equate contemporary events (the fall of Assyria to Babylon) with the Dragon battle:

> 3) Yahweh is slow to anger and of great forebearance,
> but Yahweh does not remit all punishment.
> He travels in whirlwind and storm
> and clouds are the dust of his feet.
> 4) He rebukes the sea and dries it up,
> and he makes all rivers fail. (NA. 1: 3-4)

In the light of the foregoing mythic itinerary followed by Isaiah, Habbakuk and Joel, we can hazard a fair guess at what a better preserved Book of Nahum would contain.

* * * *

The *detailed* incorporation of the Baal mythos in the royal cultus, (which we have here, for the first time, indicated), if at all explicable in a Monotheist context, is so with reference to the most iterated word, the leitmotif of all the texts — Tsedeq, a concept of which Baal's battle with Leviathan is the detailed ideogram. Just as El was naturalized into Hebrew theology in consideration of his implications of totality and omniscience, Baal would be acceptable insofar as he represented "Just Order".

At this point the outlines of the One God have emerged like a new constellation in the heavens of Canaanite myth. If we have assessed them correctly, something comparable and corresponding should emerge when we consider the land of Canaan.

Chapter Three

The Center

We shall here be considering the Symbolism of the Center — perhaps the richest and most palimpsestic of religious Symbolisms, and very logically so: it is the archetype of the place where everything comes together, connects and interpenetrates.

We shall here offer some very general assertions about the Center, which could only be satisfyingly supported by a copious cross-cultural documentation, showing its characteristic features worldwide in the mythology of mountains, paradises, enchanted gardens, temples royal palaces, &c. Such would be beyond the scope of this study.[30] We ask the reader to accept our presuppositions provisionally and see if they are not substantiated by the materials we shall examine.

The Center will have most or all of the following features:

It is described as *the geographic center of world*, signalized by the presence of the most august mountain, the world-tree, the fountain which feeds all rivers, &c.

It is *the point of origin*, the original home of the first ancestor, the first land to rise from the waters of primordial chaos — in short, the original and oldest place. (Later this concept includes the idea of the place where the First Time can be renewed.)

The primal paradisal condition still obtains there: it is a place where death may not come, where the gods still communicate with man face to face, where work is unnecessary, &c.

---

30. It is provided by Eliade in Chapter 10 of his *Traité*, and Chapter one of his *Eternal Return*.

It is *the place of the world axis,* that is, the point were where Heaven, Earth and Underearth meet, where a "breakthrough in planes," travel from one world to another, is possible.

The classic Center in Hebrew mythology is of course Eden:

> 8) The Lord God planted a garden in Eden, in the east, and placed there the man whom he had formed. 9) And from the ground the Lord God caused to grow every tree that was pleasing to the sight and good for food, with the tree of life in the middle of the garden, and the tree of knowledge of good and evil. 10) A river issues from Eden to water the garden, and it then divides and becomes four branches. 11) The name of the first is Pishon, the one that winds through the whole land of Havilah, where the gold is. 12) The gold of that land is good; bdellium is there, and lapis lazuli. 13) The name of the second river is Gihon, the one that winds through the whole land of Cush (Ethiopia). 14) The name of the third river is Hiddekel (Tigris): the one that flows east of Asshur. And the fourth river is the Euphrates.
> (GEN. 2: 8-14)

We shall now systematically examine the Symbolism:

Geography: The place of the garden is the center of the world, for the rivers that define the four directions radiate out from that which rises in Eden. Only the Euphrates can be positively identified, but the mythic placement of the other streams can be inferred thus:

First, the location of Eden, "in the east," means eastward of the writer, i.e. east of Israel, probably in Babylonia (Southern Iraq). From this standpoint Ethiopian Gihon (the Nile?) is surely for the West, Tigris (Hiddekel) "east of Assyria" is East; the Euphrates which empties into the Persian Gulf is South. The remaining Pishon (the Oxus?) in Havilah must be North. (This identification of the directions, borne out by the text, connecting the account to the four principal rivers of the Ancient Near East, is new, since no previous commentary has understood that a Center symbolism is in play.)

Origin: Eden is the home of the original ancestors (Adam and Eve) who established all human customs (such as language — Adam names the animals).

Paradise: though it may seem superfluous to point out that Eden is edenic, we will note the paradisic implications of its very name, *Eden,* Hebrew for "delight." Here the world's original blissful dispensation obtains, food is had without work, animals have no fear of man and do not attack him, death is unknown.

World-Axis: this would of course be the Tree of Life, which, we note, is placed in the center of the garden which is the world-center, and has the power to confer immortality. The Tree then is as it were steeped in Center Symbolism. Its true world-axis character, however, is apparent only when we consider that in its vicinity God deals with Man face-to-face, i.e., it is a place where communication between the divine and human realms is possible.

In fact, every important feature of the Center Symbolism is present in the description of Eden. We will now show that all of these features are repeated in the other Hebrew world-centers, Zion and Sinai.

Geography

Sinai (also called Horeb), is not explicitly described as the geographic center of the world — for the simple reason that at the time the texts of the Bible received their final formulation Jerusalem (also called Zion for the mountain on which the Temple stood) had taken over that role.

But even without the honor of being called the world's navel, Sinai-Horeb possesses a world-tree *(qua* axis of communication with the spirit world — this is of course the Burning Bush of EX. 3:1) and a miraculous spring (which rises when Moses strikes the rock in EX. 7:6) Still, despite these and other features of Center symbolism to be enumerated below, Jerusalem is for the Hebrew the Center par excellence.

The fact that Eden retains its geographic Center trappings is harmonized with Jerusalem's status by naming the spring nearest (and south of) the Jerusalem Temple "Gihon" — thus assimilating the two descriptions.

The political and religious primacy of the Jerusalem Temple then accounts for the preponderance of Zionic center descriptions here and throughout this chapter, except where we deal with the theme of the World-Axis; there Sinai, as the site of Moses' revelation, could not be so displaced.

First Isaiah (c. 750-680 BC, author of Isaiah chs. 1-39), describes a Zion which is the highest point of the earth:

> 2)...The Mount of the Lord's House
> shall stand firm above the mountains
> and tower above the hills. (IS. 2:2)

The next line shows that its height marks a Center, for to it are added metaphorical rivers — the inflow of people from all the surrounding nations. The importance of this detail to Isaiah is shown by the fact he coins a new verb from the noun "river" (nahar) to express it:

> All the nations
> shall rush like rivers *(naharu)* towards it. (IS. 2: 2-3)

Now we may fairly consider these figurative streams, like the rivers of Eden, as features which define the focus of the four directions — for all the nations rush towards it as to a center.

The third section of the Book of Psalms, certainly post-Exilic and probably to be dated around the fifth century BC (300 years after Isaiah), gives us a Zion from which the rivers that define the directions continue to radiate.

> 7) Singers and dancers alike will say:
> "All my *(sc. God's)* springs are in you *(i.e.,* this is the source of all waters)." (PS. 87:7)

The spring seems to have been (from our point of view, very understandably) essential to Hebrew Coronation rites. We have this account for Solomon:

> 38) They had Solomon ride on King David's mule and they led him to Gihon. 39) The priest Zadok took the horn of oil from the Tent and anointed Solomon. They sounded the horn and all the people shouted "Long live King Solomon!" 40) All the people then marched up[31] behind him, playing on flutes and making merry till the earth was split open by the uproar. (1K. 1: 38-40)

— which may make sense of the otherwise obscure last line in the great Coronation psalm:

> He drinks from the stream on his way,
> therefore he holds his head high. (PS. 110: 7)

Some later, and quite interesting examples of the motif are Zecharaiah (chs. 9-14 2nd. c. BC):

> In that day fresh water shall flow from Jerusalem, part of it to the Eastern Sea, and part to the Western Sea, throughout the summer and winter (ZE. 14: 8)

---

31. Mt. Zion is not, properly speaking, the hill now so named on the southwest corner of Jerusalem's "Old City", but rather the Ophel ("the hump"), the southern spur of Mt. Moriah. Moriah was the site of the Temple, and now hosts the Dome of the Rock.

The Ophel, downhill from Mt. Moriah, possesses on its eastern slope the spring Gihon. Now this spring was neither within the ancient Jebusite city of Jerusalem, nor in the expanded city of Solomon and his successors. Only at the turn of the 7th century BC was its water diverted into the city, by Hezekiah, who cut a tunnel for it through 1,700 feet of bedrock. The new outlet, within the walls of the City of David, is the pool called Siloam, far south of the Ophel and of course downhill from it.

This tallies with the description of Solomon's coronation — for the people march up behind him — presumably from the spring to top of the Ophel.

Joel (6th c.?) offers:

> And in that day the mountains shall drip with wine,
> the hills shall flow with milk,
> and all the watercourses of Judah shall flow with water;
> a spring shall issue from the House of the Lord
> and shall water the Wadi of the Acacias. (JOEL 4: 18)

But for circumstantial detail and surrealistic power, nothing can surpass the 6th century Ezekiel's vision of the Temple as source of all waters:

> 1) He lead me back to the entrance of the Temple, and I found that water was issuing from below the platform of the Temple — eastward, since the Temple faced east — but the water was running out at the south of the altar, under the south wall of the Temple. 2) Then he led me out by way of the northern gate and led me around to the outside of the outer gate that faces in the direction of the east; and I found that water was gushing from under the south wall. 3) As the man went on eastward with a measuring line in his hand, he measured off a thousand cubits and led me across the water; and the water was ankle deep. 4) Then he measured off another thousand and led me across the water; the water was knee deep. He measured off a further thousand and led me across the water; the water was up to the waist. 5) When he measured yet another thousand, it was a stream I could not cross; for the water had swollen into a stream that could not be crossed except by swimming. 6) "Do your see, O mortal?" he said to me; and he led me back to the bank of the stream.
>
> 7) As I came back, I saw trees in great profusion on both banks of the stream. 8) "This water," he told me, "runs out to the eastern region, and flows into the Arabah; and when it come into the sea, into the sea of foul waters, the water will become wholesome. 9) Every living creature that swarms will be able to live wherever this stream goes; the fish will be very abundant once these waters have reached there. It will be wholesome, and everything will live wher-

ever this stream goes. 10) Fishermen shall stand beside it all the way from En-Gedi to En-Eglaim; it shall be a place for drying nets; and the fish will be of various kinds and most plentiful, like the fish of the great Sea. 11) But its swamps and marshes shall not become wholesome, they will serve to supply salt. 12) All kinds of trees for food will grow up on both banks of the stream. Their leaves will not wither nor their fruit fail; they will yield new fruit every month, because the water for them flows from the Temple. Their fruit will serve for food and their leaves for healing." (EZ. 47: 1-12)

Origin and Renewal

When the psalmist claims that Jerusalem is the true home of all Humans, he is making a spiritual version of Eden's genealogical claim:

> 1) His city is founded on the holy mountain (lit. his founda tion (is) on the mountains of holiness).
> 2) Yahweh loves the gates of Zion more than all the dwellings of Jacob.
> 3) Glorious things are spoken of you, O city of God.
> 4) I mention Egypt and Babylon to an acquaintance of mine; Philistia, Tyre, Ethiopia. (*sc.* He replies: "I know of)someone who was born there."
> 5) But of Zion it shall be said: "Every man was born there — may Yahweh preserve it!"
> 6) Yahweh will inscribe in the register of peoples that each was born there. (PS. 87: 1-6)

But a simple co-opting of Eden's status as "original home" is the exception. The rule is not the claim to have prolonged, but to renew the magic of the origin.

Regaining the Edenic condition is central to the enthronement psalms, sung at the annual renewal of the reign (for being a Canaanite style king meant entering into the whole cyclic itinerary of Near Eastern agricultural sacral kingship). Here we find a clear description of Mt Zion as the place of rebirth:

> 1) Yahweh said to my lord (*i.e.* the king),
> "Sit at my right hand
> while I make your enemies your footstool."
> 2) Yahweh will stretch forth from Zion your mighty scepter;
> hold sway over your enemies!
> 3) Your people come forward willingly on the day your
>   warlike power (is revealed),
> you are reborn (lit. "from the womb")
> like a new day (lit. "from the dawn")
> in the dew of your youth. (*i.e.*, you shine like a thing new-
>   born, like the dew at dawn),
> 4) Yahweh has sworn and will not change his mind,
> "You are a priest forever in the manner of Melchizedeq (*i.e.*,
>   the ancient priest-king of Jersualem when it was still a
>   Canaanite city). (PS. 110: 1-4)

The same concept seems to be in play in:

> 6) "But I have installed my king
> on Zion, my holy mountain!"
> 7) Let me tell of the decree:
> Yahweh said to me:
> "You are my son,
> I have fathered you this day. (PS.2: 6-7)

Though the notion of fathering or begetting is used in Hebrew as Egyptian as a synonym for adopting, the mountain defines the place as one not only of investiture but of Renewal.

Similarly Isaiah's Mount Zion is a place where time is abrogated, reversed, renewed: what Isaiah calls "the end of days", *aharit yamim* (IS. 2:2). This entails a retreat from the technological level where war was possible, a "turning back the clock."

> 4) Thus he will judge among the nations
> and arbitrate for the many peoples,
> and they shall beat their swords into plowshares
> and their spears into pruning hooks:

> Nation shall not take up
> sword against nation;
> they shall never again know war. (IS. 2:4)

The renewal implicit in the center symbolism of Isaiah's Zion is of course vastly magnified by the fact that this "end of days" is itself a new *Day*, and so uses the original tool of Genesis. The frightful brightness that flattens the planet beneath it in IS. 2: 10-22 is a louder, longer echo of the first Day's "let there be light." (This passage will be discussed in detail below under "Paradise.")[32]

---

32. The concept of renewal finds different and even more striking formulation in Isaiah's famous "peaceable kingdom" passage (IS. 11: 1-9), but as the explication of this material requires an excursus into Water symbolism, we offer it here in a footnote. Isaiah compares the paradisal condition is compared to a flood:

> 9) In all of my sacred mount
> nothing evil or vile shall be done,
> for the land shall be filled with knowledge of God
> as waters cover the sea. (IS. 11: 9)

Now water represents undifferentiated potentialities, as in the chaos-flood from which the world arises in a preponderance of mythologies including the Jewish. It is also an emblem of the state of death and dissolution (e.g. the waters of Sheol) to which things return, dissolving their contingent forms. The contradictory valuations of water, as origin and end of life, are resolved by the notion of water as the basis of renewal, destroying the old and bringing forth the new. Thus Noah's flood effaced the old and withdrew from a new world, which emerged at a Center mountain (Ararat) (cf. Eliade, *Traité*, 60-66). Isaiah's flood of God-knowledge, from which the renewed "holy mountain" arises is a precise parallel.

In Joel 3 we find a picture which supplements and clarifies this:

> 1) After that,
> I will pour out my spirit on all flesh;
> your sons and daughter shall prophecy,
> your old men shall dream dreams
> and your young men shall see visions.
> 2) I will even pour out my spirit
> upon male and female slaves in those days.
> 3) I will set portents in the sky and on earth,

There would come one final relocation of the time of the origin. Rabbinic Judaism, defining itself in terms of the Law, made Sinai the supreme center, and the giving of the Torah was valued as the "real" creation of the world: the establishment of its moral structure.

An interesting corroboration of these statements is the most persistent motif in Jewish piety, the omnipresent phrase which begins every blessing and seals any religious action: "Holy art thou Adonai, who sanctified us with your laws..." The iteration of this formula is an attempt to relive illimitably the moment of Sinai's transfiguration, to suffuse all of later life with the power of the Time of Origin.

Paradise

Isaiah made the Mount Zion of the future a Paradise, characterized by the abolition of war and full establishment of the "peaceable king-

> blood and fire and columns of smoke;
> 4) the sun shall turn into darkness
> and the moon into blood
> before the great and terrible day of Yahweh comes.
> 5) But everyone who invokes the name of Yahweh shall
>   escape
> for there shall be a remnant on Mt. Zion and in Jerusalem,
> as Yahweh promised. Anyone whom Yahweh calls will be
> among the survivors. (JOEL 3: 1-5)

The context is an unspecified fifth century invasion, depicted in Joel's preceding chapter, in language that likens it to autumn thunderstorms. The storm imagery is again suggested here, with cloudlike darkening of sun and discoloring of moon, while fire and smoke are ordinarily used as metaphors for lightning and cloud. The rains which in Joel 2: 23-27 brought about a renewal of the parched land and the knowledge that God is "in the midst of Israel" are here paralleled (if not equated) with the outpouring of Spirit.

The outpouring of spirit, here as in Isaiah centered on Mt. Zion, also suggests, in context, water. The word Joel uses for "pour forth", *shaphak,* being in non-poetic usage exclusively applied to liquids (water, molten metal, &c.). We are here confronted with a very familiar extension of water's symbolism — its power of renewal in the form of inspiration — as in the Greek Pierian spring, the well of Mimir in Norse myth, &c.

dom": a restoration of the coexistence with animals known in Eden.

> 6) The wolf shall dwell with the lamb, the leopard lie down with the kid;
> the calf and the beast of prey shall feed together with a little boy to herd them.
> 7) The cow and the bear shall graze, their young shall lie down together
> and the lion, like the ox, eat straw.
> 8) A babe shall play over a viper's hole
> and an infant pass his hand over an adder's den (in safety).
> 9) In all of my sacred mount nothing evil or vile shall be done,
> for the land shall be covered with knowledge of God as water covers the sea. (IS. 11: 6-9)

But even in comparison with this magnificent passage, or the Genesis account of Eden — which makes up in prestige what it lacks in literary elaboration — the development of Sinai as a paradisic region is impressive.

The accounts of Sinai describe a Strong Time, an *illud tempus*, before history had strained the fabric of existence, in fact a Paradise. Just as in Eden, food is obtained without effort — quail and manna fall from the sky and need only be gathered (EX. 16).

That the Israelites near Sinai have attained a condition superior to that of mortals is evident from the fact they eat the food of spirits:

> 23) So he commanded the skies above,
> he opened the doors of heaven
> 24) and rained manna upon them for food,
> giving them heavenly grain.
> 25) Man ate the bread of powerful spirits *(abiriym)*, he (God) sent them provision in plenty. (PS. 78: 23-25)

Though the Israelites do not here go naked, they achieve the unaging condition that nudity implies[33] insofar as after forty years their clothing is still new.

---

33. Ritual nudity shows one is outside the rule of profane time, that makes things "wax old like a garment"(Ps. 102: 27.)

> 2) Remember the long way that the Lord your God has made you to travel... 4) The clothes upon you did not wear out, nor did your feet swell these forty years. (DT. 8: 2-4)

and

> 4) I led you through the wilderness forty years; the clothes on your back did not wear out, nor did the sandals on your feet... (DT. 29: 4)

A further feature of Paradise is to be noted: it is *flat*. The sense behind this is that to the transcendent, to those who have attained the condition of spirits, there are no more impediments to motion — valleys and heights are the same to one who "flies" — he skims across them glib as a fingertip over a map.

This leveling of the three dimensions appears at the Lord's approach in Deutero-Isaiah:

> 3) A voice rings out:
> clear in the desert a road for the Lord!
> Level in the wilderness a highway for our God!
> 4) Let every valley be raised,
> every hill and mount be made low.
> Let the rugged ground become level
> and the ridges become a plain.
> 5) The presence of the Lord shall appear
> and all flesh, as one, shall behold —
> the Lord himself has declared it. (IS. 40: 3-5)[34]

---

34. This passage is quoted by John the Baptist in announcing Christ's approach (MARK 1:23; MATH. 3:3). The road-opening motif may be derived from an enthronement procession of the sacred king who would embody the god — such as is suggested by Psalm's 23 and 118.

Despite this citation from Isaiah, the New Testament expresses the same concept rather differently: Jesus displays his power, his attainment of the condition of spirits, by walking on water. The disciples, despite Jesus' chiding, seem to have understood (on the archetypal level) exactly what this meant, for they cried out in fear "It is a ghost!" (MATT. 14:26; MARK 7:49), i.e., one who has transcended the three dimensions of mortal existence.

First Isaiah's first vision of Mt. Zion at the end of Time had already, if less clearly, developed precisely this idea.

> 12) For the Lord of Hosts has ready a day
> against all that is proud and arrogant,
> against all that is lofty — so that it is brought low;
> 13) against all the cedars of Lebanon,
> tall and stately,
> and all the oaks of Bashan,
> 14) against all the high mountains
> and all the lofty hills,
> 15 against every soaring tower
> and every mighty wall,
> 16) against all the ships of Tarshish
> and all gallant barks.
> 17) Then man's haughtiness shall be humbled
> and the pride of man brought low,
> none but the Lord shall be
> exalted in that day.
> 18) As for idols, they shall vanish completely,
> 19) and men shall enter caverns in the rock
> and hollows in the ground
> before the terror of the Lord
> and his dread majesty
> when he comes to overawe the earth (IS. 2: 12-19)

In relation to God's exaltedness, the earth becomes a plane: not only in a geographical sense — the leveling of mountains and tall trees (IS. 2: 12-14) and the prominent features of the artificial landscape such as towers and fortifications (IS. 2: 14-15), but the moral landscape experiences a similar compression. Human haughtiness (IS. 2: 9-11) is brought low, and in a very literal way — mankind will crawl down caves and hide in holes at the terror of Yahweh's kratophany (IS. 2: 17-21).[35]

The paradox of a flat paradise which is at the same time a mountain should not trouble us. Though the images contradict each other, the

---

35. Zechariah 14: 4 ff. is probably another example of the land-flattening motif, but the text is too corrupt to be fairly called in as evidence.

meanings — spiritual ascension and Center — are complementary. Isaiah's contemporary from the 8th century BC, Micah, has

> 3) For lo! Yahweh is coming down from his dwelling place
> he will come down and stride upon the heights of the earth.
> 4) The mountains shall melt under him, and the valleys
>   widen till they're flat *(yithbaqu* — lit. "be split apart");
> like wax before fire, like water cascading down a slope
>   (MI. 1: 3-4)

— an instance of the motif which is particularly useful for the light it casts the famous image of the mountains melting at God's approach in Psalms (e.g. PS. 97: 5)

The levelling image is still current in the 7-6th centuries in the writings of Habbakuk, who gives a powerful account of God approaching Israel from Sinai which includes:

> 6) When he stands, he makes the earth shake;
> when he glances, he makes nations tremble.
> The age-old mountains are shattered,
> the primeval hills sink low.
> His are the eternal paths *(haliykoth olam lo)*. (HAB. 3: 6)

With our present insight into the leveling motif, we can also understand why the parting of the Red Sea was not equated with Baal's conquest of Yam.[36] The want of this seemingly inevitable association is

---

36. It was so equated, once, in IS. 51: 9-10

> 9) Awake, awake, clothe yourself in splendor
> O arm of Yahweh!
> Awake as in days of old,
> as in former ages!
> It was you who hacked Rahab in pieces
> and pierced the Dragon.
> 10) It was you who dried up the Sea
> the waters of the great deep,
> who made the abysses of the sea
> a road the redeemed might walk.

explicable only if we understand that an entirely other symbolism than that of the chaos-dragon is in play — that of the Center. We have already noted the paradisal dining and freedom from Time (i.e., unaging condition) that attends the Sinai-trek. To this may be added the perils of the transition from profane space to the Center[37] — which proves to be more

---

This passage hardly contradicts our argument, both because it is unique, and because it is so late (Trito-Isaiah, c. 4th-3rd centuries BC).

37. A further and integral, though for our present discussion peripheral, feature of the Center is the dangerous passage to it. The interpretation is that as one approaches the world of the spirits, one may lose one's ability to return to one's mortal state — one may "die". The most adequate and well-known example is the Symplegades — the clashing rocks through which Jason's ship must pass on his Journey to the Tree at the Center of the World, on which hangs the Golden Fleece. Parallel imagery occurs in the mythologies of Death and Initiation.

As the Exodus from Egypt is part of one continuous narrative, climaxing in the Sinai theophany, we may see in the crossing of the Red Sea (EX. 14-15), which the Egyptians do not survive, just such a "dangerous passage" as is ordinarily part of the Journey. The same idea is repeated a little later, with equal explicitness — if the Israelites touch Sinai during the theophany, they will "surely die" *(moth yumath,* EX. 19:12). Even to hear the voice of God may prove fatal, so the congregation prefers to learn God's will second-hand, from Moses (*w'al-y'daber imanu elohiym pen-namut,* EX. 20: 16)

Sinai is a scene of perilous eruptions from the spirit world, as is announced by the thunder, lightning, shofar-blasts and earthquake (EX. 19: 9-25; 20: 15-18).There is a danger that Yahweh may simply blast the Israelites out of (profane) existence *(pen-yifrots bahem,* EX. 19: 22).

A final observation on this theme will be the way it clarifies the peculiar horror at Jerusalem's storming by the armies of Nebuchadnezzar:

> 12) The kings of the earth did not believe
> nor any inhabitants of the world,
> that foe or adversary could enter
> the gates of Jerusalem. (LAM. 4: 12)

Traditionally this sentiment is explained by assertions that Israel felt itself to be God's favored possession — though no promise of impregnability was ever given. To the contrary, God's promises are typically accompanied by assertions of the dire consequences to follow the withdrawal of his protection.

than the Egyptians can survive. In the context of these cohering features, the parting of the Red Sea as part of the flattening of landscape which marks the Center is probably put beyond reasonable dispute. Walking "through" the Red Sea is, in content, entirely comparable to Jesus walking "on" the waves — an instance of the Transcendence of Space.

World-Axis

Obviously the Temple is a place where communication between the worlds of Men and Spirits can take place, but it is worth pointing out the thoroughgoing way in which this is developed in the symbolism of the Temple's altar.[38]

First there is the Bronze Sea described in 1 K. 7: 23-26. This is paralleled by a basin of holy-water in Babylonian temples, called Apsu, which is the word for the subterranean fresh water ocean, source of all life and fertility.

This bronze Sea was supported by twelve bulls, probably four groups of three, referring to the seasons or directions, a common decorative motif. This was unlikely to be zodiacal as the oldest known list of 12 zodiac signs is much more recent than this construction, and the Babylonian proto-zodiac had 17 signs.

The altar, placed higher than the Sea, is built (Ezek. 43: 13-17) in three stages, each smaller than the one below, like a ziggurat. The lowest was set on a foundation platform called *heq ha'arets*, "the bosom of the earth." The same expression, "bosom of the earth," *irat eretsiti*, was used in inscriptions by Nebuchadnezzar for the foundation platform of his royal palace and the great temple-tower of Marduk in Babylon, Etemenanki. (He follows there archaic patterns, and his work should not be taken to suggest imitation of the Jerusalem model).

Though the first two stages of the Ziggurat proper did not have names, the summit was called *'r'l,* (vocalization is uncertain), and is

---

Now, if we understand the particular dangers of the Center, an enemy's entry into Jerusalem is quite understandably "unbelievable."

38. These observations on the symbolism of the altar are all taken from Albright, Archaeology, pp. 148-152, who explores the Near Eastern parallels in somewhat greater detail.

almost certainly from the Akkadian *arallu,* which has the dual sense of "underworld" and "mountain of the gods." The Hebrew term for the altar summit, *har El,* "mountain of God," is a popular etymology which conveys the correct sense.

The altar is topped with four horns at the corners, as were the Babylonian temple-towers, the top stage of which was called *ziqquratu,* lit. "mountain peak."

These hard archaeological facts, describing a structure which is like a ladder from Underearth to Heaven, climaxing in a mountaintop, are matched by the literary record, as in Moses' encounter with the burning thornbush (EX. 3) on Mt. Horeb, there explicitly characterized as a "holy mountain" *(har ha-elohim,* EX. 3:1).

When communication between the worlds of men and spirits takes place — God here speaks directly to Moses — on a mountain top, the plant which stands at the center of the experience (the Burning Bush) is plausibly to be taken as a "world-tree" or "world-axis."[39]

Isaiah's holy mountain, Zion, is similar to Horeb — here too one attains "direct knowledge of God" (IS. 11: 9). The bridge between heaven and earth is of course implicit in the mountain itself, but Isaiah goes on to furnish us with an explicit world-tree, personified as the Messiah (which is simply the Hebrew word *Moshiah*, "anointed", a synonym for "king"), who is described in arboreal language as the conduit through which the spirit of God comes to earth:

> 1) But a shoot shall grow out of the stump of Jesse
> a twig shall sprout from his stock.
> 2) The spirit of Yahweh shall alight upon him,
> a spirit of wisdom and might,
> a spirit of counsel and valor,
> a spirit of the knowledge and reverence for Yahweh,
> 3) his sensing shall be by the reverence for Yahweh:
> he shall not judge by what his eyes behold,
> nor decide by what his ears perceive.
> 4) Thus shall he judge the poor with equity *(tsedeq)*
> and decide with justice *(mishor)* for the lowly of the land.

---

39. We might here cite Jacob's ladder in parallel, but the symbolism is there not so circumstantially realized in terms of geography.

> He shall strike down a land with the rod of his mouth
>   *(i.e., his authority)*
> and slay the wicked with the breath of his lips.
> 5) Justice *(tsedeq)* shall be the girdle of his loins
> and faithfulness *(emunah)* the girdle of his waist
>   (IS. 11: 1-5)

The iteration of tree-terms (stump, twig, sprout, stock and rod) is so consistent and thorough that we may fairly see in this an adumbration of the world-tree function, whose effect is here moral/political as much as spiritual. The messiah is the heir of the sacred king, who similarly by his *tsedeq*, *mishor* and *emunah* establishes the agricultural world-order. An interesting development is that while Baal and his stand-in the sacred king preside over a renewed year-cycle, the Messiah does so over a new Millenium. But the enhancement of scope is matched on the level of symbolism: while the sacred king was anointed *at* the center, the Messiah,[40] equated with the World Tree, has *become* the center, and, by bridging the realms of men and spirits, produced a total reintegration of heaven and earth: four lines later, the land is as full of direct knowledge of God as the ocean is of water.

* * * *

Due to the complexity of Center symbolism, we have here reversed our method, and first presented the Biblical material, reserving the Canaanite documents for the end. Having gone throught the above material, one will now encounter a passage like:

> There, she (sc. Asherah) is off on her way
> Towards El of the Sources of the Two Floods
> In the midst of the headwaters of the Two Oceans.[41]

and, with the supplementary knowledge that Aherah is here visiting El at his home on Mt Tsaphon (identified *passim* in the Baal and Kirta

---

40. Zechariah (chs. 1-8), writing in early postexilic times, 3-400 years later than 1st Isaiah, attests the enduring power of the Messiah-World Tree equation: he refers the the Messiah simply as "my servant the Branch" (ZE. 3:9).
41. ANET p. 133, e II AB (iv-v) 20-22.

Epics as the home of Baal and the gods and the site of the divine Council), know that we have here a complete center symbolism, with fountains, mountain, paradisal condition and contact with the spirit world. One is emboldened to assume that many more features were shared than those of which we have here clear record, since we have explicit identification of Mt. Zion with Mt. Tsaphon in this psalm (probably to be dated to Sennacherib's menace to Jerusalem in 701):

> 2) Yahweh is great and much acclaimed in the city of our
> God, his holy mountain,
> 3) fair-crested, joy of all the earth, Mt. Zion, summit of
> Tsaphon... (PS. 48: 2)

In the face of so clear a statement, we cannot view the three-tier altar in the temple described in the beginning of this chapter as so much window dressing. It was used, like all the details of Center symbolism we have analysed, not only for its aesthetic prestige but also for the detail of its symbolism.

And indeed, unless we take into account the profound influence of particularly Canaanite Center Symbolism, we shall be hard put to account for how a religion so nomadic in its origins and so universalist in its full development, should preserve so superhumanly resolute an attachment to a particular area of land.

Chapter Four

Asherah and Anat

Asherah

The Bible uses the name Asherah indiscriminately to mean "fertility goddess,"[42] and we shall follow it,[43] since it is not here our purpose to probe into her prehistory.

The archetype of the fertility goddess is universally susceptible to representation as a "Tree of Life," either with an actual tree or with a pole or pillar.[44] The Septuagint and Vulgate (which the King James Version fol-

---

42. The name Ashtoreth (in the Bible, synonymous with Asherah) is used in the plural as an abstract noun for "offspring" or "increase": "...the calving of your herd and the lambing *(v'ashtroth)* of your flock (DT. 7: 12, see also DT. 28: 4, 18, & 51.) On this line B.D.B. offers (p. 800, *s.v. Ashtoroth)* the precisely parallel Latin expression *veneres gregis,* "fertility (lit. 'venuses') of the flock".

Patai, in chapter 3 of his Hebrew Goddess, makes the interesting conjecture that Leah's cry of *"b'Ashri"* when she's about to give birth to Asher in GEN 30: 13 may be understood as "Please, Asherah!" — an invocation to the fertility goddess as birthhelper.

43. To clarify the mine-field of names involved:

Asherah (pl. Asheroth) is the Hebrew name for a Canaanite fertility goddess (known to us in the Ugaritic texts as Athirat). The name Asherah is also used in the Bible for Asherah's cult object.

Ashtoreth (pl. Ashtaroth) is the Hebrew name for another Canaanite fertility goddess (known to us in the Ugaritic texts as Athtart). The Bible makes no distinction between her and Asherah.

Astarte is the Greek form of the name Athtart.

Ishtar is a Mesopotamian a fertility goddess equivalent to Athtart; Asherah however is eqivalent to the Mesopotamian goddess Ashratum.

The best concise treatments of this complex topic are the articles "Asherah" (John Day) and "Ashtoreth" (Diane V. Edelman) in the *Anchor Bible Dictionary.*

44. For the representation as Tree, see Eliade, *Traité,* ch. 103, "Great Goddesses and Vegetation;" as to the substitution of pillar or pole, there are the

lowed) usually render Asherah by "grove" (Gr. *alsos,* L. *nemus),* and the Mishnah understood them to be living trees which were worshipped (Tract. 'Or. 1: 7: 8; Sukk. 3: 1-3; Abod. Zar. 3: 7, 9, 10; Me'il 3: 8). Also we have prohibitions against *"planting* an Asherah or a wooden pole beside the altar of Yahweh" (DT. 16: 21) and fulminations against the worship of the "Queen of Heaven" (i.e., consort of Baal) "under every spreading tree" which are too numerous in Scripture to require citation.

On the other hand, the Asherah is sometimes described in the Bible as a object which one "makes" *(asa)* (1K. 14: 15; 16: 33; 2K. 17: 16; 21: 3, 7; 2 CHR. 33: 3), "builds" *(banah)* (1K. 14: 23) or "erects" *(natsav)* (2K. 17: 10).[45]

As the frequent denunciations would suggest, the worship of this deity was as widespread as it was ineradicable.[46] In fact, an image of Asherah seems to have stood in the Jerusalem temple at the gateway to the altar:[47] the famous "Image of Jealousy" *(semel haqqinah)* of which Ezekiel (8:5) complains.

In the light of Asherah's career in Israel as fertility goddess and sacred tree or pole, one may be inclined to cast a suspicious eye even on

---

Inanna poles of Sumer, the Greek *Hekataia,* and the Hebrew Asheroth which will be discussed below.

45. The speckled poles which Jacob sets up at the water-trough to make Laban's flocks bear speckled lambs were probably fertility-goddess symbols. We have a trough from ancient Iraq (ANET fig. 503) with clear Inanna-poles engraved on the front that seem to echo the patriarch's expedient.

46. Patai shows in chapter 3 of his Hebrew Goddess, she was worshipped in the holy land from the first settlement, usually with Baal, in wooden images set up on hilltops, in the Northern Kingdom for as long as there was a Northern Kingdom (till 722) and beyond — the Sacred Pole of Asherah that Jeroboam (who established the Northern Kingdom of Israel in 926) set up was still there for Josiah of Judah (639-609) to burn 300 years later (2 K. 23: 15.)

In the Southern realm, Judah, Asherah was introduced into the Temple by the wife of Solomon's son Rehoboam.Ceaselessly removed and restored by successive kings, Asherah was, by Patai's calculation, present in the Temple for roughly 1/3 of the time that edifice stood.

47. The placement of fertility goddess poles, mezuzah-like, at gateways is abundantly attested for the Hekate-fetishes of Greece (AESCH. *fr.* 388 Nauck; PAUS 2: 30: 2; ARISTOPH. *Wasps* 800-04.) The Inanna-poles seem to have *evolved* from house gateposts (Wolkstein/Kramer, *Inanna,* p. 188, notes 44-45.)

Eve, "the mother of all that live", *(em kal hay)* — in GEN. 3: 20, who is so closely associated with a magic garden and cosmic tree. Similarly one may be drawn to speculate about the female figures in the *Song of Solomon,* whose "limbs are an orchard of pomegranates and of all luscious fruits" (S.S. 4: 13) and who are generally equated with a fertile landscape where "all the sheep bear twins and never miscarry" (S.S. 4: 2). But if indeed these figures play on the imagery of the earth and fertility goddess Asherah, they do so in a peripheral fashion.

When this tree-identified deity is called into play *as* a goddess figure, she is so in very clearly more-than-mortal form: as the personification of the nation — as a vine that God plucked from Egypt and whose shade covers mountains, whose boughs stretch as far as the Mediterranean and the Euphrates (PS. 80: 9-12). The resemblance to the Canaanite Venus does not end here: the relationship between God and the land that is his "Vineyard of Delight" (IS. 27: 2-6) has a very explicitly erotic dimension.

The *heiros gamos* or sacred marriage, in Canaan, Babylon, and throughout the Near East,[48] was a rite by which the king and high priestess coupled to symbolize and magically encourage the sky-god's fecundating embrace of the earth. It appears in the Deutero-Isaiah passage just noted, but had already received a even more remarkable treatment from this Isaiah's predecessor Hosea *(floruit* late 8th century BC). Hosea adapted the Canaanite rite with Dada literalness: he married a whore (chs. 1-2) to symbolize God's marriage to Israel (who had "played the harlot" with foreign gods). The final harmonizing of their union is described in language that, by turns erotic and agricultural, is quite explicitly archaic in content.

> 21) And I will espouse you forever:
> I will espouse you with Righteousness *(b'tsedeq)* and Justice
> and with Goodness and Mercy.
> 22) And I will espouse you with Faithfulness;
> then you shall be devoted to the Lord.
> 23) In that day
> I will respond
> — declares the Lord —

---

48. Eliade, *The Myth of the Eternal Return,* pp. 23-27, gives Near Eastern and worldwide examples.

> I will respond to the sky
> and it shall respond to the earth,
> 24) and the earth shall respond
> with new grain and wine and oil,
> and they shall respond to Jezreel.[49]
> 25) I will sow her in the land as my own
> and I will say to Lo-ammi, "You are my people",
> and he will respond "you are my God." (HO. 2: 21-25)

The bride espoused with *Tsedeq*, who shall be "sown in the land" has inherited the *hieros gamos* one would postulate for Asherah and Baal in some detail and with much precision of purpose. Compare this passage where Baal invites another of his consorts, the goddess Anat, to his "pleasant place" atop Mt. Tsaphon:

> "Pour peace into the heart of the earth,
> rain love on the heart of the fields."
> (Coogan *Stories*, p. 93 = ANET p. 136 C)

By the 3rd century BC, under Greek influence, steps towards what was to become a rational theology had made idol-worship no more of a real threat. Judaism was now a moral philosophy competing with the Greek moral philosophies. In this climate it was possible to engage in some fairly bold play with pagan images, and we find Wisdom characterized in explicitly goddess language. She is placed on hilltops, at doorways, at the city gates and at the crossroads, the very locations where one would encounter the goddess fetishes, the sacred poles, of the ancient near east. Wisdom is here explicitly arrogating the honors of the Greek Hekataia, the Asherot of Canaan, and the Sumerian Inanna poles:

> 1) It is Wisdom calling,
> Understanding raising her voice.

---

49. Jezreel, lit. "God sows", is the name of Hosea's son, as Lo-ruhama ("Unpitied") and Lo Ammi ("Not-My-People") are those of his daughters, by the whore. All three names are here applied to Israel: if deliberate, the puzzling gender shifts are probably intended to make the statement more abstract (Hebrew has no neuter pronoun).

> 2) She takes her stand at the top of high places, by the wayside, at the crossroads *(beyt n'thiyvoth,)*
> 3) She shouts at the gates, at the entrance of the city...
> (PROV. 8: 1-3)

> 34) Happy is the man who listens to me,
> coming early to my gates each day,
> waiting at my doorposts *(m'zuzoth p'thahay.)*[50]
> (PROV. 8: 34)

Like the fertility goddesses, Hochmah (Wisdom) confers a bountiful harvest, long life, health.

> 16) Length of days is in her right hand,
> and in her left hand riches and honor.
> 17) Her ways are pleasant ways,
> and her path conducts you to wellbeing *(shalom)*.
> 18) She is a tree of life to those who grasp her, whoever holds on to her is happy. (PROV. 3: 16-18)

Wisdom is even explicitly described as a divinity, with a temple of her own:

> 1) Wisdom hath builded her house, she hath carved for it seven pillars,
> 2) she hath sacrificed an animal, now prepares its meat for a sacred feast, pours out the wine, makes ready her table... (PROV. 9: 1-2)

The places where Wisdom takes her stand, her description as a *Tree of Life*, and her (literal) enshrinement in verses 9: 1-2, identify her as the latest incarnation of Asherah-Israel. But we cannot here more than mention the phenomenon, which opens the subject of Judaism's confrontation with Greek philosophy, and its development of a *Mythology of Reason* — which we shall take up in the next volume. For now it must suffice to have outlined Asherah's early career among the Hebrews, from

---

50. *Cf.* PROV. 1: 20 for placement at road, wall & gate. See also chapter one of our *Rotting Goddess* for a full treatment of the sacred pole and its symbolism.

popular idol and source of literary allusions, to symbol of the nation, to Bride of God. Asherah has gone from being the idolatry par excellence to the ultimate symbol of piety, of the reciprocal love of God and the Human Soul, without ever abandoning her arboreal form.

Anat

A further goddess figure among the Hebrew archetypes is one corresponding to the Canaanite war and fertility deity Anat. Anat's sanguinary and agricultural qualities are clear from:

> The gates of Anat's house were shut,
>   and the lads met the lady of the mountain.
> And then Anat went to battle in the valley,
>   she fought between the two cities:
> she killed the people of the coast,
>   she annihilated the men of the east.
> Heads rolled under her like balls,
>   hands flew over her like locusts,
>   the warriors' hands like swarms of grasshoppers.
> She fastened the heads to her back,
>   she tied the hands to her belt.
> She plunged knee-deep in the soldiers' blood,
>   up to her thighs in the warriors' gore;
> with a staff she drove off her enemies,
>   with the string of her bow her opponents.
> And then Anat arrived at her house,
>   the goddess reached her palace;
> there, not satisfied with her battling in the valley,
>   her fighting between the two cities,
> she made the chairs into warriors,
>   she made the tables into an army,
>   the stools into heroes.
> She battled violently, and looked,
>   Anat fought, and saw:
> her soul swelled with laughter,
>   her heart was filled with joy,
>   Anat's soul was exuberant,

as she plunged knee-deep into the soldiers' blood,
>	up to her thighs in the warriors' gore,
until she was satisfied with her battling in the house,
>	her fighting between the tables.
The soldiers' blood was wiped from the house,
>	oil of peace was poured from a bowl.
The Virgin Anat washed her hands,
>	the Mistress of the Peoples her fingers;
she washed the soldiers' blood from her hands,
>	the warriors' gore from her fingers.
She made the chairs chairs again,
>	the tables tables;
>	she made the stools stools.
She drew water and washed,
>	the heavens' dew, the earth's oil,
>	the rain of the Rider on the Clouds
dew which the heavens pour,
>	rain which is poured from the stars.[51]

The subject of the carnage in the house is unclear and has so far defied scholarly analysis. We would suggest, however, that we have here an equation of the bloodshed of the battlefield with the wine-shed of the banqueting hall: something very much along these lines is suggested by a myth of Hathor, whom the Egyptians themselves equated with Anat. (The translation is a little opaque in its literalness. The plot is: Re has sent Hathor to destroy mankind. Repenting, he tricks her into abandoning the task by giving her red beer in place of blood to drink.)

> So then this goddess came and slew mankind in the desert. The majesty of this god said: "Welcome Hat-Hor, who hast done for me the deed for which I came!" Then this goddess said: "As thou livest for me, I have prevailed over mankind, and it is pleasant in my heart!" Then the majesty of Re said: "I shall prevail over them as a king (15) by diminishing them!" That is how Sekhmet came into being, the (beer)-mash of the night, to wade in their blood from Herakleopolis.

---

51. Coogan, *Stories,* pp. 90-91 = ANET p. 136, B

Then Re said: "Pray, summon to me swift and speedy messengers, so that they may run like the shadow of a body." Then these messengers were brought immediately. Then the majesty of this god said: "Go ye to Elephantine and bring me red ochre very abundantly." Then this red ochre was brought to him. Then the majesty of this great god caused...[and He-With]-the-Side-Lock who is in Heliopolis ground up this red ochre. When further maidservants crushed barley to (make) beer, then this red ochre was added to this mash. Then (it) was like human blood. Then seven thousand jars of the beer were made. So then the majesty of the King of Upper and Lower Egypt: Re came, together with these gods, to see this beer.

Now, when day broke for (20) the slaying of mankind by the goddess at their season of going upstream, then the majesty of Re said: "How good it is! I shall protect mankind with it!" Then Re said: "Pray, carry it to the place in which she expected to slay mankind." Then the majesty of the King of Upper and Lower Egypt: Re went to work early in the depth of the night to have this sleep-maker poured out. Then the fields were filled with liquid for three palms, through the power of the majesty of this god.

Then this goddess went at dawn, and she found this (place) flooded. Then her face (looked) beautiful therein. Then she drank, and it was good in her heart. She came (back) drunken, without having perceived mankind.[52]

For the general association of the fertility goddesses with slaughter, a good cross-cultural parallel is to be found among the Aztecs. A certain death emphasis is integral to all such goddesses, who also represent the grave since this is an aspect of the life cycles they supervise. But the funereal is far more highly developed here, where Xochiquetzal (Precious Flower), the Aztec Aphrodite, queen of fruit, flowers, love, springtime, &c., is actually identified with Itzpalotl (Obsidian Knife Butterfly), the deified sacrificial blade.[53]

---

52. *The remainder of this story has to do with the origin of certain names and customs, such as the use of strong drink at the Feast of Hat-Hor.* Wilson trs., "Deliverance of Mankind from Destruction", ANET p. 11.

53. For an exemplary treatment of these, see Brundage, *Fifth Sun*, chapter 7.

This ambivalence is clarified by the light of Eliade's finding[54] that human sacrifice is normative for goddess-oriented agricultural religion. Hunter-gatherers see the kill as a borrowing of the flesh of a creature who is placated by the reassembly or burial of the bones.[55] The animal is a "given" in the landscape, and its taking results in myth and ritual expressing mutual obligation and respect, no thought of atonement. The harvesting of crops however is a year-long premeditated "murder": the long cultivation makes for a sense of responsibility and gives rise to myths of slain and resurrected gods the devouring of whose flesh originates the use of a staple food.

Cannibalism, head-hunting, human sacrifice, &c. are ritual reflections of agricultural myths, and as such not found among hunter-gatherers. Human sacrifice is not a primitive or "wild" act, but *cultivated* behavior.

In this context the equation of agricultural production with bloodshed, and the ambiguous account of Anat's "Feast" become understandable. We are now prepared to cast a very knowing eye on the text of Joel's (5th century BC) apocalypse. This vision explicitly describes the return of rain in autumn (which is equated — chs. 2-3 — with the onset of an unspecified foreign war). Joel continues the imagery with a depiction of the harvest-home which draws heavily on the archetype we have just discussed:

> 9) Proclaim this among the nations!
> Consecrate yourselves for holy-war!
> Arouse the warriors,
> let all the fighters come and draw near!
> 10) Beat your ploughshares into swords,
> the blades of your pruning hooks into spear-heads.[56]
> Let even the weakling say: "I am a man of valor!"
> 11) Hurry and come!
> all the nations are gathered there.
> Bring down, Yahweh, your warriors!

---

54. In chapter two of *History of Religious Ideas*, vol. 1.

55. For a fine example of this motif, see the Micmac legend "Bringing Back Animals" in Whitehead, *Stories from the Six Worlds*, pp. 66-68.

56. The echo of Isaiah 2: 4, written about three centuries earlier, must be deliberate.

12) Let the nations rouse themselves and march up to the
valley of Yehoshaphat[57]
for there I will sit in judgement[58]
over all the nations round about.
13) Swing the sickle
for the crop is ripe;
come and tread
for the wine press is full,
the vats are overflowing
for great is their (the nations') wickedness.
14) Multitudes upon multitudes
in the valley of Judgement,
for the day of Yahweh is at hand
in the valley of the verdict.
15) The sun and moon are darkened
and stars withdraw their brightness.
16) Yahweh will roar from Zion,
and shout aloud from Jerusalem,
so that heaven and earth tremble.
But Yahweh will be a shelter to his people,
a refuge to the children of Israel.
17) And you will know that I, Yahweh, am your God,
who dwell in Zion my holy mount.
And Jerusalem shall be holy,
never more shall strangers pass through it.
18) And in that day
the mountains will drip with wine,
the hills shall flow with milk. (JOEL 4: 15-18)

The paradigm of agricultural violence is invoked in line 10 with the inversion of Isaiah's phrase, and horrifically continued to the point where the Valley of Yehoshaphat is filled with blood like a vast wine-vat — eerily reminiscent of Hathor's blood-colored beer which covered the earth to the height of three palms.

In Israel, the harvest comes immediately before the onset of the autumn rains — this is taken account of in Joel's apocalypse, by refer-

---

57. This refers to the valley in 2 CHR. 20 where the righteous 9th century Judaean king Jehoshaphat gained a victory over Israel's neighbors.
58. Heb. *yishpot,* a play on the valley's name.

ences to the clouds (darkening of sun and moon) and thunder (Yahweh's shout that makes heaven and earth tremble).

The same atmospheric phenomena concluded Anat's slaughter quoted above:

> She drew water and washed,
> > the heavens' dew, the earth's oil,
> > the rain of the Rider on the Clouds
> dew which the heavens pour,
> > rain which is poured from the stars.

Post-exilic Trito-Isaiah picks up the image of the bloody harvest in:

> 1) Who is this coming up from Edom,
> from Bozrah in garments (stained) purple —
> who is this, majestic in attire,
> pressing forward in his great might?
> "It is I who make good what I say, powerful to rescue."
> 2) Why is your clothing so red,
> your garments like his who treads grapes?
> 3) "I trod out the vintage alone,
> no one, of all the world's peoples, assisted me.
> I trod them down in my anger,
> trampled them in my rage.
> Their life blood spurted on my garments
> and all my clothing was stained.
> 4) For I had planned a day of vengeance
> and my year of redemption arrived.
> 5) Then I looked, but there was none to help.
> I stared, but there was none to aid.
> So my own arm saved me,
> and my rage — that sustained me.
> 6) I trampled peoples in my anger,
> I made them drunk with my rage,
> and I hurled them to the ground. (IS. 63 1-6)

In these examples from Joel and Isaiah Yahweh has assimilated the attributes of Anat, indeed gone beyond the Canaanite and even

Egyptian materials in archaic content: for the butchery is *explicitly* equated with a harvest.

It is one of the paradoxes of the archetypes that, as they degenerate in the direction of literature, as in the Ugaritic epics or those of Homer, the outline of the Symbolisms remains vaguely, repeated without clear comprehension of content. But once the desacralisation is complete, when the images may be used as "mere metaphors" for a later, more sophisticated religious idea (here Yahweh as He who directs History) — then the archetype, because it has been relegated to the unconscious, recovers its details and full articulation. Logically: the "poetic imagination" is a far freer medium for the archetype than the ever-fossilizing (if fossil-durable) context of living religious tradition.

Asherah and Anat were then apparently both assimilated to the Yahweh mythos, the one to account for his love, the other to explain his rage. It seems that to the two principal goddesses of Canaan was entrusted the task of embodying the entire emotional life of God.

Due to the complexity of the material and the novelty of our approach, we have so ar refrained from tracing the Canaanite material further into Jewish religious literature. We shall make an exception in this case, because of the momentous nature of the influence.

Indeed, it would have been easy enough to do the same for the earlier figures taking *only* the best known source, the classic of Kabbalah, the 12th century *Zohar*. There we find El ensconced (as *Hokmah*, "Wisdom")[59] among the topmost spheres of the Cosmos; the Baal mythology continues to provide motifs for Yahweh, the Messiah, and the Apocalypse; the Kabbalistic Tree of Life is perhaps the most grandiose example of Center Symbolism; but Asherah and something very like Anat, now named Shechina and Lilith, surpass them all.

Shechina, became the very dryad of the Tree of Life, and, (from the 16th century on) occupied the place of honor in formal religious thought, while Lilith, who has more than a little in common with Anat (though no direct lineage) is the lead character in folk religion for the same period.

---

59. Not to be confused with the goddess of the same name who appears in the Book of Proverbs.

But this is matter for another book.[60] It is enough for us to have shown that these goddesses were siezed upon and adapted as emblems of the Love and the Terror of God.

60. Daniel Matt's *Zohar*, Tishby's *Wisdom of the Zohar*, and (for the background in Midrash) Bialik & Ravnitsky's *Book of Legends* provide authoritative and fully annotated access to all this material in English.

Conclusion

What we hope to have achieved in this volume is a demonstration that Canaanite and other Near Eastern mythologies were drawn on by the Hebrews in a deeply coherent, selective, and adaptive way. Despite the impression given by modern Bible scholarship, that the Scriptures are a patchwork of forgotten fables, we find in them a very directed collective effort, motivated by a single overriding concept or inspiration.

Out of the whole menagerie of Canaanite gods, only El, Baal, Mt. Tsaphon and Asherah/Anat, were meaningfully drawn on, and these as ideograms of God's Omniscience, Justice, Omnipresence, and special love for Israel. This book is the first to acknowledge the full extent of Canaanite influence, and the only one to note the systematic abstraction of the myths into symbols of a moral philosophy.

We feel that this view of the material accounts more economically and less ingeniously for the facts than any other so far advanced. In volume two we hope to show that it was the Mosaic concept which so successfully directed the collective mind of the Hebrews for the thousand years we have reviewed, and gave this mastery of the very seductive cultures of its neighbors.

Even now, at the halfway point of our project, when we have done no more than lift the flowering vines of imagery that overgrew the inner structure of the early Jewish religion, we feel that more than a first step has been taken, not only in assisting Biblical scholarship to take a more integrated view of the material, but perhaps even in reviving the mummy that is modern Judaism.

Scientifically speaking, religion is not "real" and does not "work". To claim otherwise is to insult both the intelligence and the moral sense. But setting aside also the claims of religion to be politics or psychology or even — what people really tend to mean when they insist on the importance of religion — a sort of interior policeman to keep people from behaving too badly — we maintain that religion has value as both Poetry and Philosophy — that is, as tools by which we can understand

and experience the world as meaningful. (This is not to exclude the possibility that religion may have value and power of another sort, which it would be inappropriate to discuss in a work of scholarship.) It is on these levels of Poetry and Philosophy that the archetypes we have discussed may *demonstrably* be shown to have been the lifeblood of the Jewish religion. From the Prophets, through Talmudic legend, into Kabbalah and Hassidism: at every point of self-renewal the Jewish people have returned to their Symbols and Archetypes, and found in them the power to reintegrate the sacred with a historically altering secular by creating new forms.

> "Where there is symbol, there is creation," said Mallarmé. Quite obviously, poetic knowledge grasps the essential. But it will have taken dozens of years and unceasing research for the statement dear to Mallarmé to have begun to be understood. — Mircea Eliade, *Journals*, vol. III, p. 51.

Hopefully the reader will now be in a position to join Eliade in validating this declaration.

It must also be stressed that the archetypes are not merely Poetry, but also Philosophy. They contain concepts — and the Hebrews have shown themselves, from the beginning, masters at isolating and refining their content on this level. In Jewish hands the archetypes became images of the world, philosophies in the palm of one's hand, whose contemplation, comprehension and veneration reliably suffused life with significance, and made it actively livable. As Nietzsche puts it

> Pay close attention, my brothers, whenever your spirit tries to speak to you in Symbols — therein is the deepest source of your strengths.
> — Nietzsche, *Zarathustra*, Part One, "On Generosity."

And to be made privy to the meaning of the tribe's religious symbols which contain the essence of its Poetic and Philosophic wisdom, in the purest and most archaic sense, an *initiation*, a becoming Human.

Appendix — Literary Renderings

In the body of this book, we illustrated our points with the standard (JPS) translation. To have provided a literary rendering in that context would have been tendentious. Here we may indulge in a more artistic treatment, which will not only complement but complete the earlier work, for the material in question is also poetry: thus an important part of the content must be understood on the level of beauty. A literal rendering, which aims at conveying the bare sense of the words, cannot fully achieve the accuracy at which it aims, for it is, necessarily, aesthetically incomplete.

Our method here will be first to provide a poetic and interpretive translation, incorporating as much as possible the material ordinarily put in footnotes, so that the reader may at once comprehend the full implication of the lines.

The text will be followed by a commentary, not to explain the lines, whose meaning should be quite clear, but to defend them. Not everything will be spelled out. In most cases the reader should be able to, by consulting the Hebrew or a trustworthy literal translation, immediately see where an idiom has been paraphrased or an anachronistic equivalent employed to convey the meaning.

Notes are supplied where something of the literary or cosmological background had to be inserted into the English to show what was implicit in the Hebrew. Also, we list the emendations made to the Hebrew, and interpretations made of vexed lines, in keeping with the context, but without perfect certainty. In these cases as well, we will note only the real difficulties, trusting the reader's common sense.

The texts reflect, for the most part, an adoption of Canaanite mythology — which was used much as Milton employed classical mythology in his Christian epic. We have been at considerable pains to make clear what was in play, but the reader is also encouraged to enjoy Coogan's Stories from Ancient Canaan, *which give a quite reliable and very readable translation of the complete corpus of Canaanite myth.*

The italic superscriptions to the passages are capsule descriptions of the mythic or ritual referents. In these we use the names Yahweh-Baal and Yahweh-Anat to indicate the assumption by Yahweh of Canaanite deities' attributes and actions.

Isaiah 6: 1-7

In the year King Uzyahu died I saw Yahweh seated on his high exalted throne, so huge that the train of his robe covered the whole floor of the Temple.

Blazing, dragon-like seraphim hovered above him, and each had six wings — two folded modestly over the genitals, two to fly with, and two to shield his eyes from the glare of God

Three flashes of lightning accompanied the word they repeated to each other thrice:

"Bright, bright, bright!
is the Holiness of Yahweh
who leads the army of stars across the night sky —
every day he fills the earth with the sunlight of his splendor."

As I stood there listening at the entrance of the Temple, I saw how the thunder of their voices made the pillars of the entrance shake and filled the building with dark storm-clouds.

I thought: "Now I'm going to die, I can no longer live as an ordinary human, because although neither I nor my people are ritually or morally pure — I have no personal or inherited merit — I've dared look at the face of Yahweh, king of the sun moon and stars."

But one of the storm-spirits flew to me, and in that seraph's hand was a pair of tongs holding a coal he'd taken from the altar.

Like a bolt of lightning, he struck my mouth with the coal, and said "Touching your lips with this I cause that guilt, which is the price of the merely human condition, to leave you — all your sins are atoned for. Now you may speak with God."

Notes to Isaiah 6: 1-7

The high point of Yahweh's storm-god identification coincides, naturally enough, with the high point of Kingdom period poetry — in Isaiah. In a passage which, to this day, dominates the liturgy of the synagogue, the poet presents a complete Baal-theophany. The clear meaning of the words has been so long and deliberately squelched that considerable glossing is necessary.

> 1) In the year that King Uzziah died I beheld Adonai seated on a high and lofty throne, and the skirts of his robe covered the whole floor of (lit. filled) the Temple.

If the edges of the Lord's robe fill the Temple, the robe itself must be so huge its train covers the whole floor. This is of course to stress the immensity of the one who wears the robe — if the vision is nothing less than a complete sky-wide thunderstorm impossibly contained in the finite space of the Temple, this prologue is an appropriate way of preparing the reader for the spatial paradoxes to come.

> 2) Seraphs hovered over (lit. stood above) him. Each of them had six wings: with two he covered his face, with two he covered his legs, and with two he would fly.

A seraph is in fact a storm-serpent. The word *seraph* is an ordinary term for serpent (e.g., NUM. 21:6), and the word's root S-R-PH means "to burn". The serpent may have developed its name from the verbal root due to its poison or its gleaming appearance. In either case, the concept of "blazing" or "burning" is embedded in the word, and at a level which was clear to the ordinary Hebrew speaker (the way the English word "serpent" suggests "creeping thing" to the Latinist.)

Serpents are archetypally associated with water and often viewed as inhabitants of the cloud-realm. Think of the celestial couple of Voodoo, the rainbow-serpents Damballah and Aida Wedo, the dragons of Chinese art, or the Aztec Quetzalcoatl (lit. "plumed serpent").[61]

The "legs" of the seraphim covered by the second set of wings are here, as commonly, a euphemism for the genitals. Covering one's private parts was an injunction most strictly enjoined for the Levites serving in the Temple (EX. 20: 26; 28: 42-43). Another pair of wings will facilitate flight. The wings that cover their eyes are to protect them from the glare

---

61. For Quetzalcoatl, the most exotic of our examples, see Brundage, *Fifth Sun,* pp. 104 ff.

of God — as their three-fold cry, rightly interpreted, will make clear.

> 3) And one would call to the other
> "Bright, bright, bright *(Qadosh, qadosh, qadosh),*
> the Lord of Hosts!
> His glory *(k'vodo)* fills the earth!"

The meaning of *qadosh* is primarily "bright", though in Rabbinic times it comes to possess the normative meaning of "holy". The inappropriateness of reading the word as "holy" is clear. "Hosts," *ts'vaoth,* means "army or troop, either of soldiers (which the traditional reading joins us in rejecting) or of the stars. The latter and only possible reading matches the sense we offer for *qadosh*. Likewise the word for glory, *kavod,* can mean either weight, glory, or wealth. *Kavod* in the sense of "glory" has, like the English word, simultaneous implications of honor and radiance. These too fit in with our *qadosh* as "bright."

> 4) The pillars of the entrance would shake at the sound
> of the one who called, and the House kept filling with
> smoke.

If Isaiah sees the "pillars of the entrance" literally "foundations of the threshold" *(amoth hassipiym)* quake as he watches the seraphim, he must be standing outside the sanctuary, looking in.

> 5) I cried:
> Woe is me, I am lost!
> For I am a man of unclean lips
> and I live among a people
> of unclean lips,
> yet my own eyes have beheld
> the King Yahweh of Hosts."

> 6) Then one of the seraphs flew over to me with a live
> coal, which he had taken from the altar with a pair of
> tongs. 7) He touched it to my lips and declared:

"Now that this has touched your lips
your guilt shall depart
and your sin be purged away."

At this point we have enough details to draw the image together:

God is being very clearly presented in the imagery of Baal: the "smoke" (i.e. thundercloud) that fills the Temple, the "voice" (i.e. thunder) that shakes the pillars, and the "live coal" (i.e. thunderbolt) are all attested, *with identical figurative terminology* in the Baal-hymn turned psalm (PS. 18: 7-14) — which also pictures the storm-theophany taking place *in a temple (heykal)*.

The Seraphim or "fiery serpents," whose archetypal associations are with cloud and sky, likewise fit well with this interpretation, as very explicit personifications of thunder and lightning: their voice shakes the temple and fills it with dark clouds, while the word they thrice utter, "bright" is a verbal transcription of three lightning flashes — from which even they must shield their eyes with their wings.

The awesome *coherence* of the imagery being established, we can proceed to its meaning. In the context of a thunderstorm, we may read Isaiah's being "touched" or "struck" (the word has both meanings) by a coal from the storm-god's altar in the hands of a thunder-serpent as an account of the prophet's being (symbolically) struck by lightning. Among the Eskimo being thunderstruck is a sign of shamanic election, i.e., it means that one has put off the profane human condition ("died") and is now able to communicate with spirits.[62] Precisely such a transformation is described for Isaiah who is now no longer "unclean," i.e., profane, and may henceforth speak with God.

Despite the power and prestige of this passage, it is not a very meaningful enhancement of the Baal concept, nor is it a very grievous paganisation of Yahweh. Isaiah has here taken a motif already on hand in Psalm 18, but has used it to introduce a different and not directly related idea — that of purification as a prelude to prophecy.

---

62. Eliade, *Shamanism*, pp. 19, 55, 81,100 & n., 206.

Isaiah 24:1 — 27:1

According to the Canaanite myth which is satirized in this "apocalypse," the severe heat of the Near Eastern summer is the reign of Mot, the lord of Death and Drought, who has slain Baal, lord of Life and Rain. In the Autumn the thunder which begins the rainy season announces Baal's resurrection. The reborn storm-god kills Mot (the name means "Death"), then defeats Leviathan, the chaos-dragon of the ocean. Baal's first battle was based on the sudden change in the landscape from dusty to flooded: the second one, with Leviathan was probably inspired by the sight of the thunderstorms coming in from the Mediterranean: from Israel's coast they can look very like the sky at war with the sea.

It is more than likely the events the Ugaritic epic relates were reflected in ritual activities on earth, particularly an "enthronement procession" to a temple where the king, as representative of Baal, would be reconfirmed in his rule for the next year, thus ensuring Baal's commitment to make the land fertile for another annual cycle. A harvest festival was surely a part of the festivities, and the present Autumn holidays of the Jewish Calendar, Rosh HaShannah *and* Sukkoth *are evidently Monotheist replacements and modifications of the season's more traditional holidays.*

24: 1-13
(Summer: the reign of Mot)

It's high summer now, the season when they mourn for Baal, the
    time when Yahweh comes punishing the planet.
Everyone flees the heat — it looks like things have returned to
    primordial chaos:
see how Yahweh empties the earth, unpeoples it, inverts it, makes
    everything its opposite!
All the settled people — uprooted, scattered.
The hereditary high-priest suffers, the same as the peasant;
the slave, the same as his master; the serving girl's served the same
    as her mistress;
buyer and seller, lender and borrower, debtor and creditor —

meaningless distinctions
when the earth is deserted, sacked, left bare, picked clean
because Yahweh's passed sentence upon it.
The land is bleaching under the sun, pales as if sick with sorrow,
the world wears out, dries up, discolors:
noble, commoner, all fade under the heat.

It isn't just the time of year — it's the time of Reckoning!
The land was desecrated under its inhabitants! They broke God's
    holy law, they twisted the statutes
till the Eternal Covenant, the promise the rains would fall in season,
    the agreement between heaven and earth, was annulled.
That's what kindled this heat! Do you dare expect you'll see clouds
    again?
That's why hot haze eats at earth like a curse. The guilty with their
    land are drubbed under sunlight.
That's why the world burns all punishing summer, why so few still
    walk these streets of endless August.
The new wine meant for Autumn dries up at its source: the very
    vines have withered.
The ones who partied the most can now only groan.
No more, the drum and harp of gladness, the gatherings noisy and
    joyous — they're done.
No more the toast and drinking song. It's too hot to drink now if
    there were wine.
The city's chaotic busiment's over, all motion broken off,
    the houses are shuttered against the sun. None go out, doors
    stay closed as if they were barricaded.
The silence of the streets is like an unvoiced keening for the wine
    that was.
All delight has altered and gone, earthly happiness went into exile,
nothing's left in the city but its own emptiness.
Silence, like an impalpable destroyer, broke inaudibly in through
    the city gates —
this devastation didn't occur, just appear
here in the center of the world, in the midst of nations, in

Jerusalem, earth's heart!
Now it's bare as a tree when the fruits have been shook down,
    as a field after harvest, where scavengers have stripped what the
    reapers missed.

24: 14 — 20
(Return of the Rains: Yahweh-Baal reclaims the world)

Then the thunderstorm raises its voice in Yahweh's exalted
    sky-heights,
the echo roars back glad across the Mediterranean:

"Glorify Yahweh with lightning flashes out over the Greek Islands,
let sky-flame jag out the signature of Yahweh, God of Israel!"

We hear the sound of the storm as far off as earth's edge,
a song of praise uttered in thunder, calling "Glory to righteous
    God!"
whose laws control the rainfall
guarantee the seasons and watch over humankind!"

I said: Oy vey! Now we're in for it!
You thieve and cheat and steal, men of earth,
so God set up for you Terror and a Pit and a Net!
The one who runs from the Terror of news and rumor will fall into
    the Pit,
and if he climbs out of that, he'll be snared in the Net.
There'll be no escape when the windows of heaven open for the
    flood to rush down.
The earth's foundations will shake, the world break up,
the land will crumble, the whole planet stagger,
    swerve out of orbit, reeling like a drunk, shaking like a lean-to in a
    hurricane!

Am I talking about Autumn thunderstorms, the return of the
    rain-god Baal? All that's just an image, a likeness

of what's coming down on you with the weight of your sins. All will
    fall and none get up.

It shall come to pass on that Day that Yahweh, shouting from the
    clouds and spraying rain, will punish the gods on high,
like Baal returning to retake his throne from Mot the lord of Death
    and Drought —
but this will be no fable, and the godlings Yahweh disciplines will be
    the kings of the earth!
And all the imprisoned, the chained ones in their dungeons —
    Yahweh will remember their case.

Then the heavens will blacken with stormclouds, the moon turn red
    — with shame,
the sun itself darken, dismayed,
when Yahweh shows his power, exerts his just kingship from
    Jerusalem's temple mount
adored by the people's leaders.

25: 1 — 12
(Harvest Festival and the Defeat of Mot)

Yahweh, you're my god. I extol you and I praise you.
You plan then you wondrously achieve, loyal and true from of old.
You make a city into heaps of rubble, a fortified capitol — ruins.
You bring proud citadels to such demolition they'll never again be
    rebuilt.
And so even empires will honor you. Assyria, ruler of all the cruel
    nations along the Tigris and Euphrates, will fear you too,
because you're a refuge to the poor, to the ones with nothing left.
You're like a shelter in a rainstorm, a shadow that saves from the sun;
for the threats of tyrants are like a winter squall, like the heat of the
    desert,
but you bring them down from the heights of their pride. They
    aren't gods. Their words aren't wind — just breath.
You annul them from above, as a cloud shades out angry sunlight —

so instantly, so easily, do you silence the tyrant's brag.

Yahweh, who marshals the stars like an army, will make a rich feast
    on this mountain, this Zion, for all the world's people.
a feast of old wine, precious wine, pure and perfect wine.
Atop this mountain he'll tear away the veil that darkens all our eyes,
    the film of fear that dimmed the vision of all the nations of the
    world —
like the impalpable blindfold a condemned prisoner already seems
    to feel.
Like Baal in the myth, Yahweh will destroy Death — he'll eat
Assyria
    and wipe the tears from every human face.
Then he'll take away from earth the disgrace of having submitted to
    tyranny. Yahweh has spoken it — it will come to pass,
and on that day everyone will say:
"It's the hand of God! We hoped in him — he saved us!
It's Yahweh who was our true hope! And now we dance and laugh
    with joy;
he rescued us! His mighty hand now rests on this mountain — his
    power extends across the land,
crushing under it, like straw, Moab our enemy in the south,
    threshing Moab like straw, shattering and scattering.
As a powerful swimmer splits the water before him with
    outstretched arms,
he'll make Moab's forts and walls fly apart, to fall — all of them —
    down to the dirt.

26: 1 — 12
(Enthronement Procession of Yahweh-Baal)
On that day this song will be sung in the land of Judah:

"We have a powerful city,
walls and towers that will save us!
Open the gates
for the victory procession of Yahweh's people,

the enthronement of the nation that worships God —
the god of rain, the god of Justice;
a people who understand that Baal's thunder is only an echo of
    Yahweh,
the people of a god who protects his faithful.

"Make your plans relying on Yahweh;
he'll keep you safe — trust him!
Depend on him forever, a rock-solid everlasting basis of strength.
He sinks exalted cities with all their haughty habitants,
he humbles them, tumbles them earthwards, demotes them to dirt,
has them trampled under the feet of the poor."

The nation of God marches towards his temple:
the path is flat for these just ones, the god of Equity makes it
    level and straight.
The road God shows — by his laws and judgements — is the way
    of Life, the path to Yahweh, in whom we have always hope.
That longing for something higher which is the glory of the human
    soul — it's called "Yahweh."

My spirit within me desires God all night, waits for him as for
    dawn.
When your judgements, Yahweh, are realized on earth, the people
    of this planet learn righteousness.
When you wait — when you spare the wicked — they learn
    nothing but how further to pervert the laws.
They'll never recognize the majesty of God.
Yahweh, they'll never divine that when you draw back your hand —
    it's about to strike.
Let them see your zeal for your people, let them see their own
    shame. They're your enemies — let fire eat them up!
Yahweh, vindicate us, give us at last our loyalty's reward: you've
    already punished our sins without stint.

26: 13 — 27: 1
(Yahweh-Baal renews the world's fertility; defeat of Leviathan)

Yahweh, other kings and gods have owned us — now let us
    remember only you.
This much of the myth of Baal is true — he died.
The dead never resurrect, there are no ghosts to return.
Whom you punish, you destroy; you deaden all remembrance of them.

But you'll gather and increase your people, and they'll glorify you as
    you broaden the borders of their land.
They remembered you in their distress; when your punishment was
    on them, too weak to more than whisper, they poured out their
    prayers to you.
We were prostrate before you, like a pregnant woman about to
    birth, writhing and screaming to the pangs.
Our labor brought nothing to life. We couldn't deliver our own
    deliverance, nor could anyone else on earth.
We were dead — and you brought us back to life. Corpses, we rose
    from the ground;
asleep under earth, we woke and shouted —
you returned to us like the shining life-giving rain. The dead land,
    the land of ghosts, brought forth.

Now comes the storm. Go my people, back into your homes, bolt
    the door against it,
hide yourselves for a moment, until the wrath be passed.
Behold, Yahweh's punishing the planet for the people's sins.
No crime will stay hidden — the earth itself will show the blood
shed over her,
    the ground refuse to hide the bodies of the murdered any more.

And on that Day, Yahweh will punish his enemies, the other nations,
    as Baal did Leviathan, that quick-slipping serpent, that great wind-
ing snake,
    as Baal did the Dragon of the Sea with his great, sharp and powerful sword.

Notes to Isaiah 24:1— 27:1

24: 1-23: Background

This entire apocalypse is modeled on the myth of Baal, as is evident from the sequence (Summer — return of rain in Autumn — resurrection), and from the mention of specific details from the myth (e.g., Yahweh defeat's Baal's enemies Mot (Death and Drought, a personification of Summer) and Leviathan (the chaos-dragon of the ocean). What Isaiah has done is write a Yahwist parody of the Baal mythos, and we have added glossing lines to make this as evident to the contemporary reader as it would have been to the ancient listener.

Isaiah *floruit* 783-687, and saw the rise of the Assyrian empire which swallowed the Northern Kingdom in 721 and threatened to devour Judah as well. Isaiah, advisor to four Judean kings, was a prophet, but this term requires some explanation if we are to understand what he writes.

The prophets of Kingdom period were not foretellers of the future in vague apocalyptic terms, but poets and satirists who used literary symbols (like those in the Baal myth) to describe contemporary politics and morals. Certainly, Isaiah speaks for and to God, but this is not to be taken very much more (or less) seriously than the similar claims of his near-contemporaries Homer (8th century) and Hesiod (7th). Like them, Isaiah promises to reveal the divine and hidden patterns in reality, but also, like them, he understands what is and isn't real — however spiritually or figuratively he speaks. Thus our translation brings out the — to our ears — somewhat secular sense of the writing, the only way it can — by expanding the language, to make clear the implied political context. Previous translations have suffered from the double disadvantage of recognizing neither the mythological content nor the literary bias of the work, preferring to see in it apocalyptic matters which bear no relation to religious thought of the 8th century.

The scene of devastation with which chapter 24 opens will be immediately understandable to anyone who's spent a summer in Israel. The heavy heat of summer feels like a punishment from above, and whoever can flee the cities does. The deserted streets are like the after math of a military defeat.

That Isaiah does indeed mean a summer is shown by his description of the earth as *uml'la* and *navlah* — synonymous words meaning "withered, faded, sere" (24:4). Further, the inhabitants are described as *haru*, "burnt, parched" (24:6). The actual word "summer" wasn't used — because it was obvious.

In this context, the anulled Everlasting Covenant *(b'riyt olam,* 24:5) is the Covenant to guarantee rainfall which God makes with Noah — in great detail — in GEN. 8-9. The same concept appears as a major provision in God's overall covenant with Israel in DEUT. 11: 13-15, a provision so important that orthodox Jews still recite it, twice daily, as part of the *Sh'ma* (the declaration of God's oneness).

24: 1-23: Emendations and Textual Difficulties:

24:4, read, following Kittel, *hamarom im am ha-arets.*

24: 11, lit. " a crying out over the wine in the streets." The situation in the streets already described, silence and desertion, is like a soundless lamentation for the wine (i.e. revelry) which can no longer take place.

24: 14 — 23, our reading of this passage as describing a storm follows the primary meaning of the words. Sounds on high heard to earth's verge, that shake the planet, and darkenings of sun and moon, do not admit of another coherent interpretation.

26: 16, for our elaborate interpretation of *Tsaddiyq* ("righteous"), see Ringgren, *Israelite Religion,* pp. 83-84, and the use of the word in Psalms 85: 10-13 and 72: 1-7.

25: 1-12: Background

The reference to the myth of Baal (the rain-god)'s return and defeat of Mot (god of Death and Drought, a personification of Summer) each

Autumn is clear from the sequence: summer then storm in chapter 24, followed by the harvest festival in 25. It is further emphasized by puns, the twice-repeated and less-usual word for destroy used in lines 7 and 8: he will destroy *(billa* — which sounds like a verb made from the name Baal) Death *(maweth* — a word cognate with the name Mot).

The identification of Death with Assyria is supported by the lines environing these famous phrases which describe, first, a cruel foreign empire, then Judah's closer foe Moab. Given the political referents and Isaiah's date, the allusion is clear. The traditional reading of the lines, as earnest of the Resurrection of the Dead, is nonsense: this is a political satire.

25: 1-12: Emendations and Textual Difficulties

25: 10, *Madmenah* is mentioned as the site of Moab's defeat, but The associations (principal city? battlefield?) and even the location are entirely in doubt. The term is omitted, since it could only point to the dead end of this footnote.

26: 1-12: Background

Our interpretive reading of *goy—tsadiyq* (26: 2) as "the people of the god of *Tsedeq*" depends, first, on the syntax: it's a noun and adjective combined in the construct state, hence the nation of the one who is *tsadiyq* (not the possible but tortuous reading "the nation who are *tsadiyq*", the "righteous nation" we find in the standard translation. For the meaning of *Tsedeq* see the note to 24: 16 above.)

The term *Tsedeq*, which has the emphatic connotation of "regular rainfall" in 24: 16 (in the midst of a thunderstorm description!), is here too a reference to Baal, lord of Rain, and we believe an even more explicit one. It is very plausible that the ritual commemoration of Baal's defeat of his enemies was followed by a procession to his temple where he was reinstated in divine kingship (the rites of Horus are a precise parallel).

In fact, such a coronation procession is described for Solomon in 1K: 1: 38 — 40, and Psalm 24 describes a very similar coronal march, with explicit directions that the "eternal gates" be opened for the god who has put boundaries on Ocean (24: 7) — clearly a reference to the Baal mythos. To this we may add the march of God up from Sinai to defeat the Ocean Dragon in Habbakuk, which concludes its description of the landscape levelling before God with the phrase "His are the eternal paths *(haliykoth olam lo)."* (HA. 3: 6)

26: 13 — 27: 1: Emendations and Textual Difficulties

Expanding the Baal allusion in the coronation procession above, we have the puns of 26: 13 & 14. Baal's mythic resurrection, which would take place as the rains routed the dryness of Summer (i.e., of Mot), is surely satirized here, where Israel accuses itself of apostasy, saying "other lords owned us *(b'alunu)"*, and then discredits those "lords" with the phrase "the dead don't *(bal)* live again." Indeed, unless we see these words as echoes of the name "Baal" and allusions to his myth, there is no logical connection between the two lines.

Bibliography

This is of course nothing approaching a listing of the books that address the Canaanite content in the Hebrew Bible, or which have informed our survey. These are merely texts which we have more than referred to in the course of it. For those interested in seriously exploring the subject, we would recommend Coogan's *Stories,* as the most accurate and readable translation,with a fine introduction and bibliography. Ginsberg's translation of the Ugaritic texts in ANET remains the standard for super-scrupulous accuracy.

For overall interpretation of the Canaanite mythos, the best brief treatment is Eliade's in *A History of Religious Ideas,* (U. Chicago 1978) vol. 1, pp. 149 ff., which has a lengthier, critical bibliography. The *Anchor Bible Dictionary* is the most convenient way of finding a *precis* of current scholarship.

Reference Works

ABD *Anchor Bible Dictionary,* NY, 1992.

ANET *Ancient Near Eastern Texts Relating to the Old Testament,* Ed. James B. Pritchard, 3rd. ed. 1969.

BDB *A Hebrew and English Lexicon of the Old Testament,* eds. Brown, Driver & Briggs, Oxford, 1951.

Primary and Secondary Sources

William Albright, *Archaeology and Religion of Israel,* Johns Hopkins Press, Baltimore, 1956.

Burr Cartwright Brundage *The Fifth Sun: Aztec Gods, Aztec World,* University of Texas Press 1979.

Michael David Coogan, *Stories from Ancient Canaan,* The Westminster Press, Louisville, KY, 1978.

Mircea Eliade, *Essential Sacred Writings,* Harper S.F., 1991

Journal, III (1970-1978), U. Chicago Pr., 1989.

The Myth of the Eternal Return, Princeton U. Pr., 1991.

Traité d'Histoire des Religions, Payot, Paris, 1949; Eng. Patterns in Comparative Religion, (trans. Rosemary Sheed), Sheed and Ward, NY 1958. (Citations are given by section-numbers, which are the same in the English and French editions.)

Shamanism, Archaic Techniques of Ecstasy, trans. William Trask, Bollingen, Princeton, 1974.

Georg Fohrer, *History of Israelite Religion,* trans. David E. Green, Abingdon Press, Nashville/NY, 1972.

Charles G. Leland, *Algonquin Legends,* (1884) Dover, NY 1992.

Raphael Patai, *The Hebrew Goddess,* Wayne State, Detroit, 1990.

Jacob Rabinowitz, *The Rotting Goddess,* Autonomedia, Brooklyn, 1998.

Helmer Ringgren, *Israelite Religion,* trans. David E. Green, Fortress Press, PA, 1966.

N.K. Sandars, *Poems of Heaven and Hell from Ancient Mesopotamia,* Penguin 1971

Ruth Holmes Whitehead, *Stories from the Six Worlds,* Nimbus 1988.

Diane Wolkstein & S. N. Kramer, *Inanna, Queen of Heaven and Hell,* Harper & Row, 1983